THE MUSEUM OF LOST ART

THE
MUSEUM
OF
LOST
ART

INTRODUCTION

A MUSEUM OF LOST ART

Imagine a Museum of Lost Art. It would contain more masterpieces than all the world's museums combined. From the treasures of Rome to the library of Alexandria, from the religious art smashed in the Reformation to the masterpieces taken in the Gardner heist, from the looting of the Iraq Museum and hundreds of thousands of archaeological sites to the ancient structures and statues smashed by ISIS, from the hundreds of thousands of treasures seized by the Nazis to the millions of objects stolen, hidden or destroyed throughout the modern era and never found, a Museum of Lost Art provides a cutting reminder of the fragility of the world's treasures. Many of humanity's greatest artworks have been lost to theft, vandalism, iconoclasm, misfortune, and wilful or inadvertent destruction. Still more have disappeared, at the mercy of thieves, with only a sliver eventually recovered, often after dramatic investigations. It is important to study what has been lost and why, to understand how art can best be preserved in the future, to appreciate what has survived, and just how delicate is that miraculous fraction of mankind's creative history that has endured for centuries or even millennia. It is important, also, to recognize that the art blessed with survival is not necessarily the art that was most important or influential when it was first displayed. Just because an object had the bad luck to have been lost or destroyed, by man or by nature, does not mean its place in history was insignificant.

For most artists of the pre-modern era (prior to the Industrial Revolution, around 1750), only a fraction of their known oeuvre is extant, its location known. For instance, around one-third of the roughly fifteen paintings by Leonardo da Vinci that are referred to in contemporary and later written sources is accounted for; at least eight works are lost. Caravaggio painted some forty works for which we have any written evidence (as with Leonardo, the number varies among different scholars), with an uncertain number lost, ranging from eight to 115.[1]

Scholars know of many other lost works by masters such as the Athenian sculptor Phidias, the Venetian painter Giorgione and the German artist Dürer: art destroyed, stolen or simply missing. Collected, these lost works comprise a compelling negative-space history of art, for these works were as renowned in their time as their extant counterparts. Had it survived, Leonardo's monumental sculpture *Sforza Horse* would be as important as the *Mona Lisa*; Rogier van der Weyden's *Justice of Trajan and Herkinbald* was more famous during his lifetime than his iconic *Deposition*, now at the Prado in Madrid; Picasso's burned *Portrait of Dora Maar* would hang proudly beside his *Portrait of Marie-Thèrése Walter*; and the original bronze version of *Laocöon and His Sons* would outshine the Roman marble copy that holds pride of place in the Vatican Museums. Many lost works were more important and celebrated than those that have survived, but our understanding of art is skewed, inevitably, towards works that can be seen, that have outlived the numberless dangers that can befall a work of art that is often as brittle as a piece of paper. This book seeks to correct this prejudice in favour of the survivors and to resurrect and preserve the memory of the lost.

The lost works here were chosen not only because they are high-profile, feature the lost (or nearly lost) artworks of famous masters, and have fascinating stories populated with bizarre characters and plot twists. The works selected also offer an alternative history of art. Most art history today uses a core of some two-hundred or so extant historic works, illustrated and discussed over and over again. But there are lost works that, while they existed, were as important and praised as these, if not more so. The chapters to follow tell not only the stories of how many great works were lost, but also the stories behind the works themselves, what we can learn from them and how they enrich our understanding of the history of art.

A MASTERPIECE GOES UP IN FLAMES

Of all the lost art that was more important culturally, historically and in terms of influence than works by the same artist that have survived, foremost might be Rogier van der Weyden's fire-consumed paintings for the Golden Chamber of Brussels Town Hall.

We know precious little about the life of Rogier van der Weyden, one of the greatest and most influential painters of mid-fifteenth-century Renaissance Flanders. The archives of Rogier's native city of Tournai were completely destroyed during the Second World War and, with them, the secrets of the painter's early life and work. Some archival material had been partially transcribed in the nineteenth century, and it is from these fragments that we know as much as we do about the man called Maistre Rogier de le Pasture, who would later change his name to the more Dutch Rogier van der Weyden.

During Rogier's lifetime, his most famous and important work was a series of four colossal paintings, each on the theme of justice, commissioned for the Gulden Camere (Golden Chamber) of Brussels Town Hall. Unusually, two of the four works on panel, both dated to 1439, were signed – a convention that was not regular for painters until the nineteenth century, but which Rogier and his contemporary, Jan van Eyck, practised on occasion). The other two panels were probably painted later, but all were complete and in place by 1450. The bombardment of Brussels by French troops on 13–15 August 1695, during the Nine Years' War (1688–97), and the subsequent fire that raged through the city obliterated all four of them (along with a third of the city's buildings), and they survive only in numerous descriptions by visitors who admired them (including Albrecht Dürer, who in 1520 made a special point of visiting the chamber to see them), as well as several copies in drawings, paintings and tapestry. This tapestry from 1459 represents the most intact and complete indication of how the paintings looked, even including inscriptions along the edges of the tapestry that are thought to have originally been inscribed on the framing of the panels.

The paintings were each around 3.5 metres (12 ft) high, and the four spanned some10.5 metres (35 ft) across – enormous

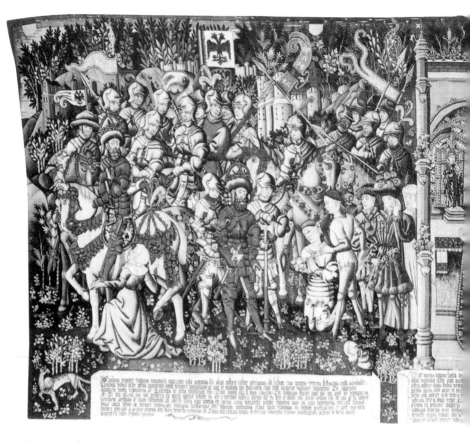

Rogier van der Weyden, *Justice of Trajan and Herkinblad*, c.1459, tapestry, 430 × 864 cm (14 ft 1¼ in × 28 ft 4 in), Bernisches Historisches Museum, Bern

Rogier van der Weyden, *Deposition*, 1435, oil on panel, 220 × 262 cm (6 ft 10 in × 8 ft 7 in), Museo del Prado, Madrid

for panel paintings, a size to rival frescoes. Their subjects were meant to provide a moral example to the judges of the Golden Chamber, demonstrating the exemplary moderation of justice by the Roman emperor Trajan and the rather more summary version carried out by the mythical Duke Herkinbald of Brabant. Paintings of famous scenes of justice being fairly meted out in Flemish town halls were popular at the time, and other renowned examples have survived: Dirk Bouts decorated the town hall of Louvain with *Justice of Emperor Otto III* (c.1473–75), and Gerard David's *Justice of Cambyses* (1498) – a particularly gruesome scene of the live flaying of a corrupt judge – looked down on the chamber of the aldermen in Bruges Town Hall.

The first panel of Rogier's *Justice Cycle* showed the emperor Trajan, mounted on a steed and setting off to battle the Dacians, stopped by a peasant woman who demanded justice, for one of Trajan's soldiers had murdered her son. As we 'read' the painting chronologically, moving from left to right, we see the murderer beheaded, while Trajan and his nobles look on (as does an anachronistic Franciscan monk). This tale comes from the thirteenth-century *Alphabetum Narrationum* ('The Alphabet of Tales') by Etienne de Besançon, though in the original, c. AD 100, Trajan offers the old woman his own son in exchange for her murdered child. The second panel sees the sixth-century Pope Gregory I praying before Trajan's Column in Rome, then examining the skull of Trajan in the presence of a bevy of cardinals while a doctor points to Trajan's tongue, which is miraculously still intact and ready to resume pronouncing fair death sentences. Akin to the uncorrupted bodies of dead saints, an emperor's ability to bestow justice never dies. The third panel shows a legendary Duke of Brabant, Herkinbald, lying ill in bed. We then see him suddenly rise from the bed and slit the throat of his evil nephew, whom he has summoned to his side and now executes for the crime of rape that the good duke felt would go unpunished if his nephew were to be tried in a more traditional manner. Another section of this panel sees the witnesses to this private execution, including the painter himself. The fourth panel also features Herkinbald in bed, while a bishop ministers to him before a huge crowd. The duke is shown miraculously receiving the Host, despite the fact that he did not confess to the murder of his nephew, believing the death to be just, not sinful. God, it seems, concurred. The panels offer up a balance of public justice, dealt out by Trajan, and private, meted out by the infirm and bed-ridden vigilante, Herkinbald. Both were considered praiseworthy secular historical examples, to be emulated by the judges who would hear cases in the Golden Chamber.

Its large scale, dozens of figures and formal complexity of this work place it alongside van Eyck's *Adoration of the Mystic Lamb* (the Ghent Altarpiece) among the crown jewels of Flemish painting in the mid-fifteenth century. Contemporaries certainly thought that they were on the same level, and both were sought out by intellectual travellers from around Europe. *The Mystic Lamb* survives to this day, despite fire, theft, iconoclasm, looting, rogue vicars, dismemberment and more, while the bombs and blazes of the Nine Years' War laid waste to Brussels and the work that was the pinnacle of Rogier's career.

It is sobering to consider how many masterpieces by renowned artists we have lost. Rogier is now best known for his *Deposition*, but during his lifetime, his *Justice Cycle* was his monument. The *Deposition* can boast an impressive influence over the centuries, held in a prominent collection, accessible to admirers, thinkers and artists. One wonders what different, maybe greater, influence the *Justice Cycle* might have had, had fortune allowed it to act as a point of pilgrimage for artists for centuries more. It is easy to forget that works we associate with great artists were not necessarily their greatest, most influential creations; often they are just the ones that happen to have survived, winning the historical roll of the dice.

LOST ART FOUND

All is not lost, though, and key to this story is a message of hope. For lost artworks, even those thought to have been destroyed, sometimes resurface.

In 2011 two lost Leonardo paintings were displayed in London at the National Gallery's 'Leonardo at the Court of Milan' exhibit, part of the list of fifteen authentic works generally agreed on as by his hand. *Madonna of the Yarnwinder* was stolen from a Scottish castle in 2003 and only recovered in 2007. *Salvator Mundi* was part of the art collection of the English king Charles I (reigned 1625–49) but disappeared, only to resurface in 2005, bought for a pittance because its owner did not realize it was a Leonardo.[2] A third work is more controversial. *La Bella Principessa*, a painting on vellum, is thought by several leading scholars to be another lost Leonardo that was mislabelled as a nineteenth-century German painting.

Leonardo da Vinci, *Salvator Mundi*, c.1500, oil on walnut panel, 65.6 × 45.4 cm (25³/4 × 18 in), Private collection; the painting was auctioned by Christie's for 450.3 million dollars in November 2017, making it the most expensive work of art ever sold

Others are certain it is not, and a famous forger, Shaun Greenhalgh, has claimed authorship, confusing things further.

An investigation began in 2007 to find a lost Leonardo fresco, the *Battle of the Anghiari*, which numerous scholars believe is hidden behind a false wall in the Palazzo Vecchio in Florence, deliberately walled in by the artist Giorgio Vasari in 1563 in order to preserve it when he was commissioned to repaint the Sala dei Cinquecento. He may even have left a clue painted into the scene, a single piece of text written on a waving flag high above floor level, which reads *Cerca Trova*, 'Seek and You Shall Find'. The search has been on hold since 2012 due to bureaucratic in-fighting.[3]

In 2010, a newly discovered crucifix thought to have been carved by Michelangelo was bought by the Italian State. Caravaggio's *The Taking of Christ* hung, grime-encrusted, in a shadowy corner of a Jesuit seminary in Dublin until it was discovered in 1987 and identified as a lost masterpiece; it is now the main tourist attraction at the National Gallery of Ireland,

La Bella Principessa, possibly a portrait of Biancca Sforza, attributed by some to Leonardo da Vinci, 1495?, chalk heightened with pen and ink on vellum, laid on oak panel, 33 × 23.9 cm (13 × 9¹/₂ in), Private collection

Top: Peter Paul Rubens, *Battle of Anghiari*, after Leonardo, 1603, brown ink on paper, heightened with gouache and lead white, 45.3 × 63.6 cm (17³/₄ × 25 in), Musée du Louvre, Paris
Bottom: Caravaggio, *The Taking of Christ*, 1602, oil on canvas, 133.5 × 169.5 cm (52¹/₂ × 66³/₄ in), National Gallery, Dublin

Dublin. These stories of seemingly miraculous rediscoveries of works thought definitively lost at once inspire optimism and help to contextualize the value of the works that do exist. Our museums are full of treasures, and it is a small miracle that so much has survived, and highlighting what has been lost helps us appreciate what endures.

FOR THE LOVE OF ART

Listing departed artworks may sound like a roll call of the dead after battle, the names carved into a memorial. That is, in fact, an appropriate parallel. Just as the name of a person no longer living acts as a placeholder for a full life story, a biography that one hopes will not be forgotten simply because the person is no more, so with the story of a painting or sculpture or building. The importance of remembering what no longer exists is amplified when we consider that these works were, for the most part, by great artists and were owned by politically and historically important individuals, and therefore played a role in the shaping of history. Each artwork was crafted with purpose and passed through numerous hands, was loved and admired (or sometimes disliked or even reviled) by scores of viewers. Each artwork exerted an influence, sometimes mild, sometimes great (consider public commissions such as Michelangelo's *David*), raising ardour in some (Savonarola, the villain of Chapter 4, on iconoclasm, was so incensed by fifteenth-century Florentine art that he ordered it burned for indecency in the Bonfire of the Vanities of 1497), love in others (Adam Worth may have kept the stolen Gainsborough *Portrait of Georgiana, Duchess of Devonshire* (1787) because it reminded him of his true love, who had scorned him for another man). This book brings back to life a selection of dead artworks, delving into the stories of some works in depth, mentioning others in passing, just as another book might offer a selected history of men and women no longer with us, but nevertheless with stories to tell – stories important to recall, since their absence means that they are too often unjustifiably overlooked, forgotten.

THEFT

A midnight in May, 1876. Old Bond Street in London is deserted. The air is warm, the sky inky and starless. Through the dark, two men walk past the galleries that line the street. One is short and tightly built, with an elegant moustache, impeccably dressed. The other is enormous, with a bulging barrel chest and a gorilla-like carriage. The two men stop in front of number 39, the office of Agnew's Art Gallery.

Agnew's was in the newspaper headlines at the time, having purchased an infamous painting – Gainsborough's *Portrait of Georgiana, Duchess of Devonshire* – for what was then the highest price ever paid for a work of art at auction: 10,000 guineas, a number that raised eyebrows the way the 140 million euros paid for Mark Rothko's 1951 *No. 6 (Violet, Green and Red)* did in 2014.[1] The portrait's subject, Georgiana Spencer, was a fashion icon famous for her beauty and a purported sexual athlete, living in a *ménage-à-trois* with her husband and his lover. She claimed much the same popular interest as her descendant, Lady Diana Spencer. Debate had raged over the authenticity of this painting, some proclaiming it Gainsborough's masterwork, others certain it was a fake. The debate only increased popular interest in the monumental canvas, and after its purchase from Christie's the Duke of Devonshire denied that it was genuine. Whatever the truth, it was the talk of the art world.

Junius Morgan, an American banker, decided to purchase the Gainsborough as a princely gift for his son, John Pierpont Morgan (after whom the investment bank is named), and had even fixed a price with Agnew's. The sale was agreed in principal, but the painting would remain on display at Agnew's for a specified period before money and canvas would change hands. Junius Morgan had an ulterior motive in acquiring the painting, beyond mere aesthetic appreciation. In the early 1870s, a genealogist had traced his family roots, and Morgan was delighted to learn that his mother, *née* Sally Spencer, was related to the noble Spencers of the estate of Althorp through a common ancestor, a sheep farmer from Northumberland called Henry Spencer. Morgan had books and charts printed up to display his newfound pedigree. He already possessed wealth and power, and now he had a foundation of aristocracy beneath them. Gainsborough's portrait of his newly

Thomas Gainsborough, *Portrait of Georgiana, Duchess of Devonshire*, 1787, oil on canvas, 127 × 101.5 cm (50 × 40 in; cut down from its original size), Chatsworth House, Yorkshire

discovered ancestor would ground his vision of himself as a member of America's aristocracy.

But it was not to be. Not yet, at any rate. For on that warm May midnight, the large beast of a man lifted the smaller man up to the first floor window ledge of Agnew's gallery. The small man used a crowbar to pry open the window just enough to climb inside. The guard on the ground floor never heard a thing.[2]

—

The desire to own rare objects of beauty and skilled craftsmanship gives artworks a value beyond the sum of their component parts. A vase is just clay and glaze, a statue just stone or wood, a painting just pigment on hemp canvas or wooden panel. The fact that artworks possess a primary value that is non-intrinsic (as opposed to, say, a gold coin or silverware, for which the value of the raw materials is not far off from the value of the finished object) is important, because an external value system is thus placed on them.

ART AS A HOSTAGE OF WAR

Art has been stolen for as long as it has had value. Early prominent thefts include the Roman Republican army's sacking of the Greek city of Syracuse (modern Siracusa) on Sicily in 212 BC. The loot brought back to Rome was prized for its beauty and pedigree: the fact that it was Greek, and that some of it was old, added to its value. Erudite Romans began collecting all they could find, with Cicero and Marcus Agrippa (Augustus' general) among the most famous early art collectors.

It is hard to imagine a war in which art has not been seized, as booty or for resale. The Crusades brought all manner of art and religious relics to Europe from the Holy Land. The Napoleonic wars were the first in which an army had a dedicated art removal unit, tasked with packing up and shipping to Paris artworks forfeited as part of armistice terms. The Second World War saw the movement of cultural goods on an unprecedented scale, certainly in the millions. A modernized version of Napoleon's art theft unit, the ERR (Einsatzstab Reichsleiter Rosenberg), acquired tens of thousands of artworks gathered in the path of Nazi conquest; some 7,000 of these were destined to feature in the Führermuseum planned for Hitler's hometown of Linz, Austria. Even today, terrorist groups help to fund their activities by looting antiquities from the earth or pillaging them from collections to sell to the West.

FROM STEALTH THEFT TO ORGANIZED CRIME

Until the 1960s, art theft was carried out by armies during times of war and individuals during times of peace. Stealth and ingenuity were the attributes of early art crimes, in the days when human guards and locked doors were the only defence mechanisms, and human vigilance was of utmost importance – and was all too easily circumvented. Stealth thefts, like that of the Gainsborough, in which criminals try to avoid detection, may be distinguished from blitz thefts, a trend current since the advent of quality alarm systems in the mid-twentieth century, in which thieves burst into galleries when they are open to the public and are therefore less secure. Favouring the blitz technique, organized crime syndicates became involved around 1960, drawn by the astronomical prices for which art was selling at auction. Art crime shifted from a relatively innocuous, often ideological crime into a major international plague. The United States Department of Justice ranks art crime as the third-highest grossing criminal trade, behind only the drugs and arms trades.[3] There are tens of thousands of artworks reported stolen each year, though the general public is only attentive to the handful of big-name museum heists that make international headlines. In Italy alone there are 20–30,000 artworks reported stolen annually, and many more go undocumented.[4]

When organized crime became involved it brought its traditional working methods to art crime, including violence. A spate of thefts along the French Riviera occurred in 1961, particularly of Picasso and Cézanne paintings and drawings, perpetrated by the Corsican mafia. The single largest peacetime art theft in history took place in 1976, when 118 Picassos were stolen from the Papal Palace in Avignon. In that instance, guards were bound, gagged, beaten and threatened with death. Art crime, once elegant and dexterous, saw the birth of its violent offspring.

As alarm systems have improved, and with the computerized defences in museums today, stealth thefts are difficult, so art thieves have turned to the criminal blitz — attack when the museum or gallery is open to the public. Thefts range from the absurdly simple (such as the 1994 theft of Munch's *The*

Scream (1893), when a man placed a ladder against the wall of the National Art Museum in Oslo, in broad daylight and under video surveillance, then climbed into the first floor window and climbed out with the painting under his arm) to a frighteningly sudden fist of a crime (the 2004 theft of another version of *The Scream* and Munch's *The Madonna* from Oslo's Munch Museum, in which masked gunmen burst into the museum, threatened to open fire and ripped paintings from their frames, damaging them).

Alarm systems only function to alert police. In the 2004 Munch thefts, police responded in about three minutes, but the thieves were gone in under two. During the 1970s, the Irish Republican Army (IRA) stole a great deal of art from Irish country homes, once by backing a truck through the living room wall, filling it with paintings and driving away. Police response time, even with the best of intentions, allows plenty of time for thieves to make a get-away, especially in rural areas.

National Gallery, Stockholm, Sweden

One example of a blitz theft, of particular cinematic verve, took place in Stockholm on 22 December 2000.[5] The sky was crisp, clear and cold as people headed off to work or for some last minute Christmas shopping. Suddenly the air was shattered with explosions. Two car bombs were detonated at different points in the city, and the police, thinking it was a terrorist attack, rushed to the bombsites. As they did so, a car drove up the only road leading to Sweden's National Museum, built on a peninsula jutting into the bay. The occupants scattered tyre spikes on the road behind them, to burst the tyres of any pursuing vehicles. The car pulled up in front of the museum, and men wearing balaclavas and carrying sub-machine guns rushed into the building. Shouting and threatening, they forced the visitors to the floor, grabbed paintings, including two Renoirs and a Rembrandt, and escaped on a speedboat that had pulled up in the bay behind the museum. In 2001, Renoir's *Conversation with the Gardener* was found during a police drug raid.[6] After a delicate sting operation in which an American FBI officer, working with Danish police, posed as a collector willing to buy the stolen art at a meeting arranged in Copenhagen, the stolen Rembrandt *Self-Portrait* was recovered in 2005; the second Renoir, *Young Parisian,* was also recovered through FBI intervention. Unusually, all those believed to have been involved in the heist were caught within a month of the theft, with ten arrests made. Unfortunately, the paintings had already been passed forward, hence the delay in their recovery. Sadly, it is unusual in the history of art theft for stolen art to be recovered and perpetrators arrested. In as few as 1.5 per cent of reported art thefts are objects recovered *and* criminals brought to trial.[7]

Rembrandt van Rijn, *Self-Portrait*, 1630, oil on canvas, 15.5 x 12.2 cm (6 × 4³/₄ in), Nationalmuseum, Stockholm

Russborough House, Ireland

A 1986 case illustrates what can happen to stolen art that is neither sold to a dubious buyer nor ransomed back to the victim. That year saw a burglary at Russborough House, a country house in Ireland that has the unusual distinction of having been robbed of its art on four separate occasions, twice by the IRA. This time it was Martin Cahill, an Irish gangster so infamous that films have been made about him. He and thirteen accomplices stole eighteen works from Russborough House, including a Vermeer, a Goya and a Gabriël Metsu. Cahill figured that he would retire on the proceeds, but he could not find the sort of criminal art collector he expected from books and films. Unable to find a buyer who did not look like a policeman in disguise, he hatched another plan. He smuggled the Vermeer and the Goya to Antwerp, where he used them as collateral for a loan of a million pounds sterling from a diamond merchant who had bought stolen gems from him in the past. The idea was that the loan would be used to buy drugs that would be sold on the street. With the profits, Cahill would pay back the loan and retrieve the paintings, employing them again as collateral in future such deals.

That was what was supposed to happen, but the diamond merchant decided to sell the paintings himself, and he did — to a Scotland Yard undercover agent, who promptly arrested him. Another work stolen by Cahill, the Metsu, was recovered when police in Istanbul raided a deal between two organized crime groups, in which the Metsu was being traded for a shipment of drugs. In total, sixteen of the eighteen stolen works were eventually recovered. A pair of small paintings by Francesco Guardi (both showing views of Venice) remain missing; according to one report, they are 'buried in the mountains', and those who knew their location have died.[8]

In the Cahill case, stolen art was used as collateral and in a barter system between criminal groups, illustrating the interconnections among drugs, arms and art. Art theft might be fun and sexy to read about and to see dramatized on screen, but its connections to the drug and arms trade, and even terrorism, are serious.

Caravaggio, *Nativity with Saint Francis and Saint Lawrence*, 1609, oil on canvas, 268 × 197 cm (8 ft 11¹/₂ in × 6 ft 5¹/₂ in), stolen from the Church of San Lorenzo, Palermo, Sicily

Church of San Lorenzo, Palermo, Sicily

Art is also stolen in hopes of selling it to morally flexible collectors. Criminal collectors are rarer than they appear in fiction and film, however, with the result that many thieves discover that the art they've stolen is too hot to shop around. At this point, if the authorities are fortunate, the criminals grow desperate and accidentally broker a deal with a policeman in disguise, as in the case of Stockholm's Rembrandt *Self-Portrait*.

Another very famous case almost had that outcome, but the work remains missing, possibly destroyed. On 18 October 1969, thieves linked to Cosa Nostra, the Sicilian mafia, slipped into the oratory of San Lorenzo in Palermo. In a classic stealth theft, they waded through the darkness to Caravaggio's huge *Nativity with Saint Francis and Saint Lawrence*, which hung above the altar. The next morning worshippers discovered the canvas had been sliced from its frame. The Italian government was so incensed by this crime, which took place in the midst of an anti-mafia crusade, that it prompted the establishment of the world's first dedicated art police force, a branch of the Carabinieri called the Tutela Patrimonio Culturale (TPC) – the Division for the Protection of Cultural Heritage. The TPC is now the most

Vincent van Gogh, *View of the Sea at Scheveningen*, 1882, oil on canvas, 36.4 × 51.9 cm (14^{1}/$_{4}$ × 20^{1}/$_{2}$ in), Van Gogh Museum, Amsterdam

Vincent van Gogh, *Congregation Leaving the Reformed Church in Nuenen*, 1884–5, oil on canvas, 41.5 × 32.2 cm (16¼ × 12½ in), Van Gogh Museum, Amsterdam

effective art crime squad in the world, and the largest, with over 300 full-time agents. It maintains a database, nicknamed Leonardo, that contains information on more than four million stolen artworks, most of which are still missing. Unfortunately, the Palermo *Nativity* remains among them.

The painting was not sold on, as far as anyone is aware, at least not at first. Rumours circulated about its possible whereabouts, fuelled by the court testimony of mafia informers. Some thought it had been stolen for blackmail, others to decorate the wall of a mafia boss. The latter suspicion grew in probability when a pair of van Gogh paintings, *View of the Sea at Scheveningen* and *Congregation Leaving the Reformed Church in Nuenen*, stolen from Amsterdam's Van Gogh Museum on 7 December 2002, was found in September 2016 on the walls of the holiday home of a member of the Camorra, the Campanian mafia. Still, the fate of the Caravaggio remains unknown. In 1996, a member of the Sicilian mafia asserted that he had stolen the work for a high-ranking boss, and in 2009 a mafia informant claimed to have been told in 1999 that it had been damaged during an earthquake while in storage in Sicily, and had subsequently been eaten by rats and pigs at the farm where it was kept. In 1979 the investigative journalist Peter Watson agreed to go undercover for the Carabinieri, posing as an art collector keen on stolen art, in the hope of being offered the Caravaggio. He was convinced it was in the possession of the Cosa Nostra contacts he made, but he never saw it – though he was offered a stolen Bronzino and a painting by Andrea del Sarto, which were recovered thanks to his intervention.[9]

The Caravaggio *Nativity* is of great importance to both the history of art and the history of art crime. Its theft prompted the establishment of the first police unit dedicated to art and changed the way authorities approached the matter of stolen art. Nevertheless, it would take several decades, and the travesty of terrorist groups profiting from plundered art and antiquities (witness the engagement that began in 2015 of the Islamic fundamentalist group ISIS with the looting and destruction of antiquities, and before that the looting of artworks in Iraq and Syria), before art crime would be taken seriously by the public and by governments. Its loss means one fewer extant Caravaggio among the very small group of works created during his brief lifetime (he died at the age of forty). Only four works were painted while he sojourned in Sicily, hoping for a papal pardon after having murdered Ranuccio Tomassoni, ostensibly over a lost game of tennis but actually in a sordid row over their mutual love interest, in which Caravaggio attempted to castrate his rival. Now only three remain.

Isabella Stewart Gardner Museum, Boston, Massachusetts

Perhaps the most famous unsolved art theft took place on Saint Patrick's Day in 1990, at the Isabella Stewart Gardner Museum in Boston. Two thieves disguised as policemen banged on the employee entrance to the museum, after hours. They claimed that there had been a disturbance and they'd been dispatched to investigate. Without confirming this, and against protocol, the night guards opened the door. They were seized immediately, bound and gagged, while the thieves disabled the CCTV cameras and wandered the museum deciding what to take. This was not their first attempt to break in. A few days earlier, with different night guards on duty, one of the thieves had banged frantically at the employee entrance, screaming that he was being attacked by muggers and begging the guards to save him. Sticking properly to the rules, the guards did not open the door on that occasion and later saw the 'victim' walking away with the 'muggers' voluntarily.

But with different guards on duty, Plan B worked. The thieves took thirteen objects in the end, including Rembrandt's *Storm on the Sea of Galilee*, Vermeer's *The Concert* and Manet's *Chez Tortoni*; also stolen were five works on paper by Edgar Degas, and Govaert Flinck's *Landscape with an Obelisk* (1638). Notable were the arguably more valuable objects the thieves ignored, like Titian's *Rape of Europa,* a Botticelli and two works by Raphael, instead opting for a Chinese *gu* vessel from the Shang dynasty. They tried to rip some seventeenth-century Dutch paintings from their frames, but when they had trouble doing so, left them on the floor, trampling them. They tried to open a glass case containing a Napoleonic battle flag of limited value compared to works they bypassed; when they failed, rather than smashing the case, they took an eagle-shaped flagpole finial

Rembrandt van Rijn, *Storm on the Sea of Galilee*, 1683, oil on canvas, 160 × 128 cm (63 × 50½ in), stolen from the Isabella Stewart Gardner Museum, Boston, Massachusetts

instead. Investigators are still puzzled by this strange pattern of overlooking famous works to target others of far less value, delicately handling some while treading on others, breaking into the museum but being unwilling to break a glass case once inside. The case remains the biggest art theft in US history, and probably the biggest property theft in peacetime history: evaluators consider the stolen works to be worth as much as 500 million US dollars.

Johannes Vermeer, *The Concert*, c.1664–5, oil on canvas, 72.5 × 64.7 cm (28^1/$_2$ × 25^1/$_2$ in), stolen from the Isabella Stewart Gardner Museum, Boston, Massachusetts

The case long ago went cold. Ransom demands were sent to the museum director in 1994, asking only 2.6 million dollars – a tiny fraction of the combined value of the stolen works. The museum authorities were up for it, and they followed instructions to publish a coded message in the *Boston Globe* newspaper. But they never heard from the thieves again, perhaps because law enforcement got involved, perhaps because it was a hoax demand. In 1997, the journalist Tom Mashberg was taken to a Brooklyn warehouse and briefly shown what might have been the stolen Rembrandt, but nothing further came of that line of inquiry. The journalist was given some paint chips, which he was told came from the Rembrandt painting; forensic analysis showed that they could not have, though they were seventeenth-century Dutch and could have come from another stolen painting. The gap of over three years between the theft and the first ransom demand suggests that the thieves originally tried to find a buyer for the works, or had a buyer but that the deal fell through, after which they turned to ransom.[10]

The specificity of what was, and was not, stolen suggests that there was a wish list of works, though criminal collectors who commission art to be stolen are almost non-existent. Of the tens of thousands of reported art thefts per year worldwide, and with art theft a millennia-old practice, historians know of only a few dozen cases during times of peace in which a theft was commissioned for a specific, well-known artwork. Theories run thick and fast: it was the IRA, the Corsican mafia, Whitey Bulger the Boston gangster, an inside job. None have brought fruit.

Édouard Manet, *Chez Tortoni*, 1880, oil on canvas, 26 × 33.7 cm (10^1/$_4$ × 13^1/$_4$ in), stolen from the Isabella Stewart Gardner Museum, Boston, Massachusetts

An impressive 5 million dollar reward for information leading to the recovery of the art has encouraged detectives, professional and amateur, to continue the hunt. In 2015, the FBI held a press conference announcing what information they had so far. There were leads that had not been previously publicized, including the fact that one of the guards on duty the night of the robbery had let an unidentified man into the museum briefly, before the man left. Also in 2015, police searched Suffolk Downs racetrack in Boston, following a tip that the works were hidden there, but found nothing.[11] But while the media seemed to think that this press conference meant they were honing in on the stolen art, criminologists pointed out that there was nothing new put forth; the FBI had struck a wall and were hoping the press conference might shakes things lose. It did not, and we are no nearer finding the stolen art. The FBI claims to know who two of the thieves were, both of whom have since died, but the whereabouts of the artworks remain unknown. The objects are almost certainly unharmed – thieves know that it is in their best interests to keep valuable artworks in good condition – but their hiding place, at this point, may be beyond the knowledge even of associates of the original thieves, and its discovery will be more a matter of luck than anything else.

—

Inside the first floor gallery, by the light of the street lamps
outside, the small man cuts the flesh of the canvas off its support
and rolls the Gainsborough painting carefully, paint side out,
so it will not crack. He hands the canvas out the window to his
colleague, then climbs down and disappears into the night.

The police were baffled. Their only clue was that the thief
was skilful and not too tall, and he may or may not have been
wearing hobnailed shoes. That small thief was the legendary
Adam Worth, widely considered the most successful criminal
in history, the so-called Napoleon of Crime and the inspiration
for Sherlock Holmes' nemesis, Professor Moriarty.

The characters of Adam Worth and Junius and J. P. Morgan
are exemplary of two Victorian archetypes: the master thief and
the master collector. Both embody a Victorian desire to anchor
one's social class. Worth dragged himself up from a homeless
pickpocket to become one of the wealthiest men in London
society, and Morgan sought to solidify his wealth and power,
with its sheen of aristocracy, by means of an impermeable *ancien
regime* foundation. While Worth used crime as his climbing
tool, Morgan used banking, but he was never known as the
most scrupulous of businessmen. There is no evidence, to my
knowledge, of Junius, or his son, John Pierpont Morgan, using
criminal means to acquire works of art, but neither is it past
them, and a good deal of their impressive collection came to
them with few or no questions asked. The great collectors of
the Victorian era did not leave a trail to link them to criminal
collecting, but it is safe to say that their sources were not
always straightforward, as buyers and intermediaries facilitated
transactions and made collectors aware of art treasures that
could be purchased, legitimately or not.

A MASTER THIEF

Adam Worth was born in Germany in 1844 and moved to Cambridge, Massachusetts, with his family in 1849. Worth grew up in the sharp class divide of that city, where the artificial American aristocracy even had its own title, the Boston Brahmin. The Victorian critic John Ruskin said, 'Now that a man may make money and rise in the world and associated himself, unreproached, with people once far above him, it becomes a veritable shame to him to remain in the state he was born in, and everybody thinks it is his duty to try to be a gentleman.'[12] Worth determined to raise himself from immigrant poverty by any means. He left home at the age of fourteen and enlisted in the Union Army at the outbreak of the Civil War, when he was seventeen. Army records indicate that Adam Worth died of wounds received in August 1862 at the Second Battle of Bull Run. But Adam Worth did not die; indeed, he was uninjured. Whether this was a simple clerical error of which Worth took advantage, or proactive deception on his part, is unknown, but Worth found his 'death' most convenient. He began enlisting in other regiments under assumed names, receiving the cash bounty for signing up, then deserting. As a bounty jumper, he even briefly fought for the Confederacy.

After the war, he moved to New York, which in the 1860s was thick with thieves and murderers. Adam Worth, however, was always the most moral of criminals. He never once participated in a violent crime and refused to work with any criminal who carried a weapon. He insisted that his brain would be better than any weapon in getting him out of a sticky situation. As Ben Macintyre wrote in his biography of Worth, *The Napoleon of Crime* (1998), 'Worth made it a rule that force should play no part in any criminal enterprise that involved him'. He held strong principles, was a dedicated friend and yet disdained the law, which he felt kept the class rift deep and wide. While no Robin Hood of good will, he never stole from anyone who he deemed could ill afford it, and tried to model himself as a good and moral gentleman thief.

In New York, Worth distinguished himself by never gambling or drinking alcohol. He began as a pickpocket, then led a gang of pickpockets. He tried to work his way up the criminal food chain, at the top of which feasted the bank robbers, royalty among crooks. He was arrested in 1864 and sent to Sing Sing prison for three years, but he escaped in a matter of weeks. He befriended Fredericka 'Marm' Mandelbaum, the godmother of New York society criminals and a master fencer of stolen goods. An underworld *saloniste*, Mandelbaum was beloved of all crooks, and took to Worth. Macintyre suggests, 'it was perhaps Marm who taught the lesson that being a real gentleman and a complete crook were not only perfectly compatible, but thoroughly rewarding.'

Allan Pinkerton, founder of Pinkerton's Detective Agency, the immediate predecessor to the FBI, wrote in 1873, 'Instead of the clumsy, awkward, ill-looking rogue of former days, we now have the intelligent, scientific and calculating burglar who is expert in the use of tools, and a gentleman in appearance, who prides himself upon always leaving a neat job behind.' Indeed, this era of vast industrial wealth – but no telephones, electricity, fingerprint identification, fast photography or alarm systems – saw the flourishing of the gentleman criminal. This was the golden age of thieves, and the thieves' nemesis was the Pinkerton Agency.

Worth progressed from pickpocketing to bank robbery, and the 1869 theft from the Boylston Bank in Boston made him a rich man. He moved to England, bought houses in London, spent time running an underground casino in Paris, dressed in the finest clothes and ran an international criminal headquarters, based at his London mansion, offering advice to other thieves. He sometimes participated himself, crime being his only addiction, but most often he delegated, planning artful robberies in Europe, England and the United States.

Adam Worth became one of the wealthiest men in London. So what led him to steal the Gainsborough painting? Worth had a criminally inept brother, John, who had managed to get himself caught on a job in Paris. John Worth was in jail, and Adam wanted to bail him out and send him packing to the United States, never to return and inflict his incompetence on Worth's criminal clockwork world. But Worth, who had been living under the name Henry J. Raymond while in England, could not bail out his brother himself without their association becoming known. Instead, he planned to steal the famous Gainsborough and ransom it back to Agnew's Gallery, in exchange for Agnew bailing John Worth out of jail. Without alarms, the theft was all too easy. It required skill and subtlety, to be sure, but before modern technological security measures not commonly used in galleries and museums until after the First World War, a stealthy thief could feast at will, with little hindrance beyond locks and guards, which could be circumvented.

But then something unexpected happened. The lawyer Adam Worth had hired to defend his brother actually succeeded, and John Worth was released from prison. Now Adam had his brother free, along with a freshly stolen Gainsborough painting worth at least 10,000 guineas.

With John out of his hair, Adam Worth hid the painting away. The media fed ravenously on the story of the theft, which was the talk of London and the art world. One journalist wrote, '[Whomever stole the painting has] accomplished a task before which Ruskin might have paled – he made known the names of Gainsborough and of Georgiana, Duchess of Devonshire, to millions who would otherwise never have heard of them. So, in some sense, he was an apostle of culture.' Eventually Worth began covert negotiations with Agnew's for the ransomed return of the painting, but they could not agree on a price and method of transaction that would not endanger Worth. Despite Agnew's continued attempts at further contact, Worth simply decided to keep the painting.

Adam Worth was finally caught and imprisoned in Belgium in 1893. When he was released in 1897, all of his assets and his second wife had been stolen by a former criminal colleague. All he had left was the Gainsborough painting, which had been stored in a Brooklyn warehouse. From being one of the wealthiest men in England, he had become a penniless convict, his only possession a stolen painting, the most valuable work of art in the world.

Exhausted physically and emotionally, although still only in his early fifties, Worth wanted to settle down with his two children by his second wife (who was now in a mental asylum); they had been living with his brother, John, while he was in prison. He approached William Pinkerton, ironically the only man he still trusted. Pinkerton had chosen not to present evidence against Worth after his arrest, evidence that would have extended his sentence. While Scotland Yard in Britain and Sûreté in France contributed their information on Worth to the Belgian police, Pinkerton remained silent. He claimed never to have been asked about Worth, but this seems unlikely. Rather, there was an admiration in opposition. Worth knew that Pinkerton repressed information on his behalf, and would never forget this act of mercy.

Pinkerton held a special appreciation for Adam Worth, and Worth, in turn, thought highly of Pinkerton. Macintyre outlines how Worth inspired Sir Arthur Conan Doyle's criminal genius, Professor Moriarity. What Sherlock Holmes was to Moriarty, William Pinkerton was to Adam Worth. William, one of the two sons of Allan Pinkerton, was head of the Chicago branch of The Pinkerton Agency and was a brilliant and brutal, but moral and thoughtful detective. Responsible for the arrest of so many figures in the criminal mythology of America, such as the Jesse James gang and Butch Cassidy and the Sundance Kid, William Pinkerton got his hands dirty, chasing criminals throughout the American West; but he was also willing to don a three-piece suit and pursue others through the back streets of Europe, offering advice to Scotland Yard and Sûreté. He admired the grit and intelligence of the criminals he pursued, and he was in turn admired, and feared, by them. Pinkerton often hired former criminals to work for his agency. He commissioned one of Worth's enemies, Max Shinburn, to write a book on safe-cracking techniques so that safe manufacturers could take precautionary measures in new designs. The book was written, but Pinkerton suppressed its publication – it was considered too instructive to risk it falling into criminal hands.

Worth wanted Pinkerton to act as intermediary in the return of the Gainsborough, after more than twenty years, to Agnew's Gallery, now run by the sons of the man who first bought the painting at Christie's. Pinkerton would not participate in anything underhanded, but he was willing to help, and he made the necessary arrangements to return the painting to Agnew's and secure a payment for Worth. Worth intended to use this to settle down with his children (who, incredibly, never knew about their father's criminality; they knew him as Henry J. Raymond, not Adam Worth). During this transaction Worth spent three days unburdening himself to Pinkerton – ironically, the only friend he felt he had left, his nemesis. The result of this odd partnership was the return of the Gainsborough, which was promptly purchased by J. P. Morgan for 150,000 dollars, following through with the wishes of his father.

Worth died on 8 January 1902, aged only fifty-six. Pinkerton published a book on Worth's criminal career, and actually became guardian of his children. He never revealed Worth's criminality to them, and later he hired Worth's son to work at the Agency.

MASTER COLLECTORS

J. P. Morgan hung his trophy painting over the mantle in his London townhouse. The Gainsborough remained with the Morgan heirs for ninety years until 1994, when it was bought by the 11th Duke of Devonshire.

For Junius and John Pierpont, the acquisition of the most talked-about painting of the times displayed the Morgan wealth and anchored their place in society. It also displayed a real, albeit distant, relation to *ancien regime* aristocracy. Wealth defined the artificial aristocrats of America, but the painting symbolized the Morgans' genuine aristocratic roots. For Adam Worth, the possession of the painting, in many ways the zenith of what a consumer can purchase, was proof of his own worth. He held captive what high society lusted after, what money could not buy. Its high-profile history has made this portrait, if not crucial to the history of art, certainly influential in the history of art collecting.

Still today, there is little social pressure to avoid potentially questionable artworks. Buying stolen or looted art is too often forgiven as a *faux-pas*, rather than acknowledged as a crime. This attitude becomes clear when, for example, famous collectors such as such as Lawrence and Barbara Fleischman are photographed proudly for the catalogue of their antiquities collection exhibited by the Getty Museum, entitled *A Passion for Antiquities*; in the photograph of their apartment is an ancient fresco that scholars have verified was looted from Pompeii.[13] The art trade is too opaque, too international, too much of a closed gentleman's club for legislation in one country, or even throughout the European Union, to have much effect in tightening it against trade in stolen works. It would require a social campaign, like the successful movement to vilify those who wear fur, to shame collectors shown to have bought stolen art – art that has been proven to fund organized crime and even terrorism. Until this occurs, the demand for art – hot or not – will remain as high as ever, to the delight of thieves everywhere.

WAR

October 1860 in Beijing's Old Summer Palace, the air cool with the hint of the winter to come. At the stroke of noon the fantastic water clock that stands before the Haiyan Tang palace gushes forth fountains from twelve bronze heads representing the signs of the Chinese zodiac: snake, horse, sheep, monkey, rat, ox, tiger, dragon, pig, dog, rooster, rabbit. A pall of smoke begins to settle over the water, and all around, flames are lighting up the sky.

With the end of the Second Opium War in 1860, a joint British-French army was charged with ensuring that imperial China opened its borders to trade with the West. Led by James Bruce, 8th Earl of Elgin (son of Thomas Bruce, who bought the Parthenon Marbles from the Ottomans when they ruled Athens) and his superior, General James Hope Grant, French troops arrived in Beijing first and occupied the Summer Palace, followed soon after by British soldiers. The armies stripped the palace of souvenirs and valuables, unhindered by opposition forces, while British and French officials set off for what they assumed would be the Chinese surrender negotiations.[1] Lord Elgin had brought along his own public relations man, Thomas William Bowlby of *The Times*, in what was one of the earliest instances of war journalism, though the friendship between the two men ensured that Bowlby's dispatches would not be particularly objective. He described the Chinese as 'effete and faithless Mandarins', and his enthusiasm for Chinese culture, their 'admirably cultivated gardens', was balanced with his joy at the power of British weaponry, which dealt 'perfectly awful wounds'.[2]

Five times larger than Beijing's Forbidden City and seven times larger than Vatican City, the Old Summer Palace was an architectural jewel, its vast halls decked with the finest art of centuries past. Its imperial gardens stretched across 860 acres (*c.*350 hectares), and hundreds of structures dotted the landscape: temples, mazes, outdoor perspectival paintings, aviaries, a theatre, man-made lakes spanned by ornate bridges, galleries, pavilions, fountains and manor houses. Some were designed in 1747 by visiting Western architects, the so-called Western Mansions, totalling about 5 per cent of the area, but most of the complex was rich with buildings in architectural styles from around China, a showcase for the cultures ruled by the Qing dynasty. Construction of the Summer Palace began in 1703 under the Kangxi Emperor (reigned 1661–1722) as a gift to his fourth son, the future Yongzheng Emperor (reigned 1723–35), who expanded it further from 1725. The Yongzheng Emperor added several *tableaux vivant* follies, of the sort made famous in the late eighteenth century by Marie Antoinette at Versailles: the Courtyard of Universal Happiness was a *faux* village staffed by palace workers pretending to be villagers and shopkeepers, with whom the imperial family could interact; in the Crops as Plentiful Fields, eunuchs working for the royal family pretended to be happy farmers.[3] The Yonzheng Emperor also introduced the waterworks by which the Summer Palace would be best known: its centrepiece was a clock fountain that graced the largest of the palaces, the Haiyan Tang, ornamented with twelve bronze animal heads representing the Chinese zodiac; every two hours water sprayed from each head in turn, and they all simultaneously emitted a gushing a fountain at noon.

General Hope Grant had arranged for the auctioning of thousands of objects looted during the Opium Wars, with specified percentages going to officers, soldiers and even the families of fallen troops. But the looting at the Summer Palace was on a scale that surprised even seasoned veterans, including Garnet Joseph Wolseley, who later wrote a book about it:

Drawing of the formal European gardens and pavilion in the Old Summer Palace in Beijing, showing the zodiac water clock with bronze animal heads, before 1860

If the reader will imagine some three-thousand men, imbued with such principles, let loose into a city composed only of museums, he may have some faint idea of what Yuen-ming-yuen looked like after it had been about twenty hours in possession of the French ... The ground around the French camp was covered with silks and clothing of all kinds, whilst the men ran hither and thither in search of further plunder, most of them, according to the practice usual with soldiers upon such occasions, being decked out in the most ridiculous-looking costumes they could find, of which there was no lack, as the well-stocked wardrobes of his Imperial Majesty abounded in curious raiment. Some had dressed themselves in the richly embroidered gowns of women, and almost all had substituted the turned-up Mandarin hat for their ordinary forage cap. Officers and men seemed to have been seized with a temporary insanity; in body and soul, they were absorbed in one pursuit, which was plunder, plunder.[4]

But parading about in women's clothing to let off steam was just the start of it. Wolseley continues:

A mine of wealth and of everything curious in the empire lay as prey before the French allies. Rooms filled with articles of vertu, both native and European, halls containing vases and jars of immense value, and houses stored with silks, satins and embroidery, were open to them. Indiscriminate plunder and wanton destruction of articles too heavy for removal commenced at once.

Wolseley blames the French (as might be expected of an Englishman), but soldiers of both nations probably participated. He is right that once looting begins, it is difficult to curb, as 'soldiers are nothing more than grown-up schoolboys', and the 'wild moments of enjoyment passed in the pillage of a place lives long in a soldier's memory'. The wounds of the victims of that pillage fester even longer.

The looting might have ended there, but the delegation thought to have been negotiating the surrender were instead seized by the Chinese and tortured to death, including Elgin's friend Bowlby. Outraged, the earl ordered the complete destruction of the entire Summer Palace complex, 'to mark, by a solemn act of retribution, the horror and indignation [over] the perpetration of a great crime'. He also had his own reputation in mind: 'What would *The Times* say of me, if I did not avenge its correspondent?'[5]

Burning the Old Summer Palace took several days in October 1860, but this was not the last incident in which it was defaced: during Mao Zedong's Cultural Revolution (1966–76), Red Guards attacked the ruins with knives.[6] It was not until the 1990s that Chinese leaders began to encourage citizens and schoolchildren to visit the remnants of the Summer Palace, using it as a rallying point for national unity with the narrative 'this is what Europeans did to us', and emphasizing that only strong leadership will prevent this sort of thing from happening again. Little remembered by the English and the French, the destruction of the Summer Palace remains active in the Chinese imagination, stoking fury to this day.

—

LOOTING

Looting whatever could be found was still an officially sanctioned method of payment for British soldiers at the time of the Opium Wars.[7] It had also been so for Napoleon's forces, and the Napoleonic Wars were the first in which surrender of art was a requisite for ceasefire. The 1792 Modena armistice was the first in modern times to specify the handing over of a certain number of art treasures as terms of the treaty.[8] Napoleon's own love of art (he liked works that were as large and as realistic as possible) and his use of the forced surrendering of art to exert his dominance over those he defeated (they not only lost control of their land, but also had to forfeit the treasures that they deemed most valuable) were augmented by advice from Dominique Vivant Denon, first director of the Louvre after part of the royal residence was converted into a museum in 1793. Denon made a wish list of works for his ideal museum, and Napoleon's soldiers set out to fill it: the *Apollo Belvedere, Laocoön and His Sons*, Van Eyck's *Adoration of the Mystic Lamb* (the Ghent Altarpiece), Rubens' *Raising of the Cross* and Raphael's *Transfiguration,* among hundreds of others. The first known military unit devoted to art theft was founded under Napoleon, charged with seizing art from captured territories, packing the artworks and shipping them back to Paris. Seizure of art from the defeated was nothing new. From ancient Rome to the Crusades, art was valued plunder, but Napoleon seems to have been the first to institutionalize it. Lose to his army, and you will lose your art, to be gathered by a special division of officers dedicated to the subject.

The rules of life and law during times of war and in zones of conflict are based on who is in power at any given moment, and it is not surprising that art should go missing, be damaged or destroyed during times of tumult. In sanctioned, official looting, such as was employed by Napoleonic forces during the Italian campaign (1796–97), the occupying power, through official channels and means, seizes art to be used for the support of its cause; it is gifted for political gain, sold for capital, seized as a trophy of war for display.

Apollo Belvedere, second century AD, marble, H: 224 cm (88¼ in), Musei Vaticani, Rome

Top: Jan and Hubert van Eyck, *Adoration of the Mystic Lamb* (Ghent Altarpiece), 1423–32, oil on panel, 350 × 460 cm (11 ft 5¾ in × 15 ft 1½ in), St Bavo Cathedral, Ghent
Bottom: Peter Paul Rubens, *Raising of the Cross*, c.1609–10, oil on panel, 460 × 340 m (15 ft 1 in × 11 ft 1¾ in), Rome Cathedral of Our Lady, Antwerp

Raphael, *The Transfiguration*, 1516–20, oil on panel, 405 × 278 cm (13 ft 3¹/₂ in × 9 ft 1¹/₂ in), Pinacoteca, Musei Vaticani, Rome

Looting in the Ancient World

As ancient Roman generals paraded captured chieftains and other slaves during their triumphs, so too did they parade inanimate symbols of conquest. The general Lucius Cornelius Sulla dragged home the columns from the Temple of Zeus in Athens in 86 BC, to be erected in the temple of Jupiter on the Capitoline Hill. In AD 70, treasures stripped from the Temple of Herod at Jerusalem were showcased in Rome in a special display of the booty from the Jewish War, the trophies commemorated in relief sculptures on the Arch of Titus and Vespasian. Key objects were preserved as souvenirs of the conquest, while the rest were sold off or melted down to pay for the reconstruction of the city after the great fire of 18–19 July AD 64. An outdoor sculpture garden was built by the Portacus Octaviae in Rome between AD 79 and 81 to display statues taken in war: works by artists such as Lysippus, Phidias and Praxiteles, the cream of fifth- and forth-century BC Greek sculptors. All are now lost, looted in the various sacks of Rome that took place during the fifth century AD. These are instances of institutionalized looting sanctioned by the victorious regime. Displaying artistic treasures that would stand for generations was a more lasting and more elegant way to demonstrate

Relief showing Roman soldiers carrying loot from the sacked Temple in Jerusalem during the Jewish Wars, including a menorah, silver trumpets and what some have interpreted as the Ark of the Covenant, *c.* AD 81, marble, L: 382 cm (12 ft 6 in), Arch of Titus, Rome

Antoine-Chrysostome Quatremère de Quincy, *Olympian Jupiter*, from *Le Jupiter Olympien, ou l'art de la sculpture antique ... et l'histoire de la statuaire en or et ivoire chez les Grecs et les Romains*, Paris, 1814, colour lithograph

conquest than, for example, the briefly gruesome display of the severed heads of one's opponents.

The statue of Zeus at Olympia, sculpted by the Athenian master Phidias and completed by around 430 BC, was a cult statue created to stand inside the temple. A wooden internal framework was covered with ivory plates for the skin of the god and gold for his clothing and his throne, a combination of materials described as 'chryselephantine'. Phidias was said to have been inspired by a passage in the *Iliad:* 'He spoke, the son of Cronos, and nodded his head with the dark brows/and the immortally anointed hair of the great god swept from his divine head, and all Olympos was shaken.'[9] The second-century AD writer Pausanias describes the enthroned statue as crowned with olive wreaths and wearing a golden robe decorated with reliefs of animals and lilies. In his right hand was a smaller chryselephantine statue of Nike, goddess of victory, and his right clutched an eagle-capped sceptre. Zeus sandals were also of gold; they sat on a footstool carved with a relief of the battle with the Amazons. Phidias had built the now lost Athena Parthenos, a huge chryselephantine statue that stood within the Parthenon on the Athenian acropolis. The seated Zeus was much larger, as Strabo noted: 'It seems that if Zeus were to stand up, he would unroof the temple.' Its likeness survives only on coins minted around the Elis region.

There were early concerns about the conservation of the statue. The marshy land on which the temple of Zeus was built led to an innovative, though not necessarily effective, measures to protect the ivory: the locals kept the statue moist with olive oil, which also filled a shallow basin around the base of the statue. The basin also functioned as a reflecting pool that, Pausanias wrote, made the statue look twice as high.[10] The Zeus was universally admired: the Greek author Dio Chrysostom stated that 'a single glimpse of the statue makes a man forget all his earthly troubles', while the Roman author Livy wrote in the first century BC that when the Roman general Aemilius Paulus, saw it, he was 'moved to his soul, as if he had seen the god in person.'[11] Apparently even Zeus himself approved, as Pausanias tells that Phidias prayed to Zeus to show whether the statue was to his liking, and just then 'a thunderbolt fell', damaging the floor at a place where, at the time Pausanias saw it, a bronze jar had been placed to cover the hole.[12]

The Roman emperor Caligula (reigned AD 37–41) had designs on the statue, one of many that he ordered taken from their sanctuaries and brought to Rome, where their heads could be removed and replaced by his likeness. Fortunately, he was assassinated before this could be done. Lucian of Samosata, a second-century AD writer, implied that the statue was looted from the temple and taken to Constantinople: 'They have laid hands on your person at Olympia, my lord High-Thunderer, and you had not the energy to wake the dogs or call in the neighbours; surely they might have come to the rescue and caught the fellows before they had finished packing up their loot.'[13] In AD 391, the Christian Roman emperor Theodosius I banned paganism and ordered all temples closed. Georgios Kedrenos, an eleventh-century Byzantine writer, wrote that when the statue of Zeus was taken to Constaninople it was installed in the Palace of Lausus, only do be destroyed in the fire that ravaged the building in 475.[14]

The Sack of Rome, 1527

While organized armies may keep careful track of plunder as an economic tool and a cultural currency, others may release their soldiers to pillage whatever they can, either as a bonus, or in lieu of payment, or simply because the generals lack sufficient control to prevent it. The 1527 sack of Rome took place against the wishes of the ostensible head of the army, the Habsburg Holy Roman Emperor Charles V, when the 34,000-strong mercenary force, which had not received pay in some time, mutinied and forced their immediate leader, Charles III, Duke of Bourbon and Constable of France, to march towards Rome, where they would strip the city of whatever they could to extract their pay with interest. Charles was unable to prevent them from entering the city, much less able to supervise the resulting pillage, and in any event, he was killed shortly after entering Rome.

The soldiers were followed by others looking for loot. Cardinal Pompeo Colonna, part of the advancing army and a nemesis of the resident pope, Clement VII (reigned 1523–34), entered the city trailed by throngs of peasants from his personal properties, men who were eager to avenge the sacking of their homes by soldiers of the Papal Army. When Charles III's replacement, Philibert of Chalon, commanded that the destruction end, three days after it had begun, he was ignored. The looting continued for a month, resulting in the destruction or disappearance of innumerable treasures – whatever was left or had been accumulated after previous attacks on the city in 390 BC, AD 410, 455, 546 and 1084.

The Vatican Library and holdings within the Leonine Wall that surrounded the Vatican were largely left alone, thanks to the fact that Philibert made the Library his headquarters while in the city, but even this space was not immune. Two early globes, one terrestrial and one celestial, made in 1477 by Nicolaus Germanus, disappeared. Costing an impressive 200 ducats and made just two years after the Vatican Library was established, the globes are recorded in a 1481 inventory as having been displayed in the Salle Pontifica, but they vanished during the sack. Their likeness survives thanks to copies that were made for Isabella d'Este, Marchesa of Mantua, in 1505.[15] A celestial globe was part of a Greek statue of Atlas holding the world on his shoulders, dating to the Hellenistic period (323–31 BC); it survives in the form of a second-century AD Roman copy called the *Farnese Atlas*. Islamic craftsmen made terrestrial globes, and a Persian astronomer called Jamal ad-Din is said to have brought one to the court of Beijing in 1267, but these do not survive. With the disappearance of the Nicolaus Germanus works, the earliest extant terrestrial globe, made by Martin Behaim and Georg Glockendon, dates to 1492.

National Museum, Baghdad, 2003

While well-controlled armies and occupying governments may dispose of art and monuments in a calculated manner, the chaos of war zones means that other, unofficial instances of looting and destruction often take place. Individual soldiers and civilians may pocket art as a crime of opportunity. This type of looting took place during the Iraqi conflict in 2003 at the National Museum in Baghdad, when some 15,000 objects disappeared over the course of a few days. According to investigations by Colonel Matthew Bogdanos, a US Marine officer, some looting was a crime of opportunity, as passers-by grabbed small, portable artefacts out of broken vitrines. But the removal of most of the objects appears to have been premeditated. Larger objects were carefully sawn into more easily carried pieces, and objects that were in storage and had to be sought out suggested that insider knowledge of their location had been obtained well before the opportunity to steal presented itself.[16]

CONFISCATION

War churns society and turns clean waters turbid. Those with status can be cast down, families may flee or be forced into exile, and this means that art, like people, may simply disappear. During the Second World War, much art, particularly but not exclusively that owned by Jewish families in Europe, was sold to fund escape, or was confiscated on spurious grounds. Such was the case for an ethereal painting by Gustav Klimt, *Portrait of Trude Steiner* – an early work from 1898, before Klimt became the toast of Viennese society. Jenny Steiner, mother of the girl portrayed, fled Vienna in 1938, just after the Nazis took control of the city on 12 March. The painting was seized, ostensibly in lieu of tax payments, though there is no record of whether the Steiners indeed owed anything; it is unlikely that they did. Such pretenses were a common Nazi tactic to take things they had targeted. The painting's path after its seizure is cloudy, but it

Gustav Klimt, *Portrait of Trude Steiner*, 1898, oil on canvas, 140 × 80 cm (55 × 31¹/₂ in), presumed destroyed

was sold at auction in April 1941 and has not been seen since. This ghost of a painting is all the more haunting as it was a posthumous portrait of young Trude, shown aged thirteen – a ghost of a ghost.[17]

But better the unknown fate of *Portrait of Trude Steiner* than certain obliteration. The collection of Serena Lederer (Jenny Steiner's sister, both of them *née* Pulitzer) contained many works by Klimt, all of which were confiscated by the Nazis when she fled Vienna for Budapest in 1940, hoping to remain just ahead of the Nazi tide. The Gestapo packed up her family collection and moved it to a looted art storehouse, Schloss Immendorf castle, one of many such treasuries where the Nazis planned to store valuables until the war's end. But on 19 March 1945 Hitler made his infamous 'Nero Decree', specifying that anything of value that could not be defended against the rampant Allies should be destroyed, so as not to fall into enemy hands and bring benefit to them. Hitler had in mind factories, industry and food stores; he was a great lover of art, and it is not clear whether he meant that gems from among the hundreds of thousands of artworks seized by the Nazis, largely through their art-and-archive theft unit, the ERR (Einsatzstab Reichsleiter Rosenberg), were also to be burned. There is some evidence that this was not the case, for Hitler's secretary, Martin Bormann, tried to stop August

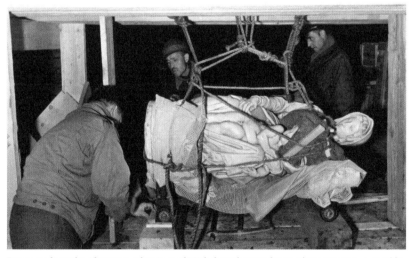

Recovery from the Altaussee salt mines of Michelangelo's *Madonna of Bruges*, 1501–4, marble, H: 200 cm (79 in); photograph, 1945

Eigruber, a Nazi *gauleiter* (local governor) who was in charge of the looted art storage facility located in an ancient salt mine at Altaussee, Austria, from blowing up the mine. It contained over seven thousand of the most valuable looted artworks, including Michelangelo's *Bruges Madonna* (1501–4) and Jan van Eyck's *Adoration of the Mystic Lamb* (c.1432). Eigruber was determined to follow through with his interpretation of Hitler's decree, whereas Bormann thought that Hitler wanted the mine sealed against the Allies, its entrance blown up, but the works inside preserved. It was only thanks to heroic efforts on the part of Austrian miners working with the Resistance that Eigruber was foiled, and the art was saved.[18]

Other treasuries were not so lucky. By 7 May 1945, with Hitler already dead and in the face of an unstoppable Allied approach, Schloss Immendorf was put to the flame by the SS, and with it scores of artworks, including fifteen works by Klimt. There is always a remote possibility that some of the art got away, however. A 1946 police report states that the night before the castle was to be blown up, SS officers 'held orgies all night in the castle apartments'.[19] The rather methodical decision to blow up the castle, the appreciation even the Nazis had for the art inside, and the fact that time was allowed to enjoy a final party at the castle before its detonation, suggests that some of the works contained there might have been secreted away before explosives were set on the building's four fairy-tale towers. The castle burned to ash, and word filtered back to Vienna that none of the works survived. This, sadly, may be the case, but hope and conspiratorial murmurings might suggest that such a report is just what opportunistic SS officers would want us to believe.

Perhaps a few Klimts are waiting to be found in some as yet undiscovered equivalent of the Munich apartment of Cornelius Gurlitt, the German art collector whose father, Hildebrand Gurlitt, had been a Nazi who dealt in looted art. When Cornelius was investigated in 2012 for tax evasion, his apartment was found to be packed with lost art: 1,406 lost works,[20] including pieces by Matisse, Chagall, Dix, Renoir and Monet. Gurlitt died in 2014 and bequeathed the collection to the Kunstmuseum in Bern – an interesting decision, to move the works outside of Germany to Switzerland. After much debate in the media about the morality of accepting a gift of looted art, the museum decided to accept the gift, provided nothing was contested by a past owner. (Several works were contested and were returned, and the museum is cooperating with any future claims.) This sort of unlikely mother lode offers hope that other such hidden treasuries of vanished works might still be out there.

COLLATERAL DAMAGE

When objects are clearly of great value, it stands to reason that great efforts should be taken to preserve them, even if they change hands. It is better for a thief, and for posterity, to get away with an unharmed work of maximum value than a damaged one that is worth less, both as a trophy and in financial terms. There is reason to hope that stolen works, such Klimt's *Portrait of Trude Steiner* or the zodiac heads from the Summer Palace, may resurface, and were preserved well while in captivity.

Other treasures suffered from collateral damage that all parties would have liked to avoid. The logistics of absconding with a painting or a small sculpture are reasonably straightforward. With the infrastructure of an occupying army at one's disposal, taking large bronze zodiac sculptures or even a 1,500-kilogram (1.6-ton) altarpiece like Jan van Eyck's *Adoration of the Mystic Lamb* (stolen completely or in part on six different occasions) can be done.[21] But what of an entire room? It sounds like an illusionist's disappearing act, and the idea that a room can vanish has inspired countless novels and conspiracy theories. The true story of the Amber Room is one that most probably finished in tragedy, but for which a modicum of hope prevails nevertheless.

The Amber Room
Amber – fossilized tree resin that feels like gemstone and comes in luscious honey and warm wood hues – has been one of the most valuable trading commodities since Neolithic times.[22] Gathered on the shores of the Baltic Sea, the material was so central to trade that the route between the Baltic and the Mediterranean has been called the 'Amber Road'. The Roman

writer Pliny the Elder (AD 23–79) passes on a report that amber gathered on the Baltic Sea was being traded by Germanic tribes along routes that saw it exported throughout the Mediterranean. He discusses its semi-mythical origins, including the belief that it was a 'liquid produced by the rays of the sun; and these rays, at the moment of the sun's setting, striking with the greatest force upon the surface of the soil, leave upon it an unctuous sweat, which is carried off by the tides of the Ocean and thrown upon the shores of Germany',[23] but he ultimately provides his own scientific explanation, that amber is the sap of a particular species of pine, hardened by the sun, sea or frost.

Besotted with both its beauty and its expense, the capricious Sophia Charlotte, second wife of Frederick I of Prussia (reigned 1701–13), encouraged her husband to order a room for their palace panelled exclusively and entirely in thinly sliced amber veneer. The original date of the commission is unknown, but the room was incomplete and uninstalled on 25 February 1713, when Frederick died; Sophia herself had predeceased him in 1705. Their son, Frederick William I (reigned 1713–40), was focused on statesmanship and war and chose not to complete the project. He presented the panels to Tsar Peter the Great of Russia in 1716 as a tactical diplomatic gift, preceding an alliance between their two kingdoms against Sweden.

Transporting the panels was no easy task: eighteen purpose-built crates were built to transport the amber panels to Peter the Great's Summer Palace in St Petersburg. But while the tsar surely appreciated the gesture, he did nothing with the panels, and they remained in their boxes for twenty-seven years. Empress Elizabeth (reigned 1741–62), daughter of Peter the Great and Catherine I, finally ordered the panels installed in January 1743 at her new Winter Palace in another part of St Petersburg. On six different occasions over the course of the next twelve years, she would have the Amber Room disassembled, enlarged and installed in a new location within the palace. In 1755, she had it relocated to a different building altogether, the Catherine Palace in Tsarskoye Selo, a section of the town of Pushkin, just south of St Petersburg. It is not clear how large the much-expanded room was at this point, nor its original intended size. It was like a living organism, expanding at the will and purse of its owners, sometimes abandoned and nearly forgotten, at other times fed to fatten.

In 1762, Elizabeth's niece came to the throne as Catherine the Great (reigned 1762–98), and decided to redecorate the palaces at Tsarskoye Selo to make them her own. This involved another renovation of the Amber Room, which by this point was an imperial status symbol, a showpiece for visiting dignitaries. Catherine purchased some 400 kilograms (*c*.900 lbs) of additional amber, at huge expense, and summoned craftsmen from Italy to work it. An oft-quoted description of the room a century later gives some sense of the phenomenon it must have been, and why it has been called a wonder of the world:

Hand-coloured photograph of the Amber Room as installed in the Catherine Palace, Tsarskoye Selo (Pushkin), near St Petersburg, 1931

Only in *The Thousand and One Nights* and in magic fairy tales, where the architecture of palaces is trusted to magicians, spirits and genies, one can read about rooms made of diamonds, rubies, jacinth and other jewels ... Here the expression Amber Room is not just a poetic hyperbole but exact reality ... The eye ... is amazed and is blinded by the wealth and warmth of tints, representing all colours of the spectrum of yellow – from smoky topaz up to a light lemon.[24]

The expanded version of the room somehow survived the turbulence of the Russian Revolution and, ironically, was wounded more by the addition of central heating than by wars and political havoc. A report from June 1941 bemoans the fact that the amber had been improperly conserved and the central heating at the palace had made it so brittle that it could not be dismantled without the panels breaking apart.

When the Second World War began, the room was so famous that it could not avoid being a target for the oncoming Nazis, and plans were made to move it eastwards by train, with most of the treasures from the palaces. But in September 1941, when the Nazis swept into Tsarskoye Selo, it was still in place, so the palace staff created a false room inside the Amber Room, lined with muslin and hessian, hoping to disguise what lay behind the new upholstery. This ruse failed, however, and when a curator from the Catherine Palace returned there in April 1944, four months after the Red Army recaptured it, he was confronted with 'a terrible site of fire. Naked brick walls covered in soot. Neither floor nor ceilings have survived. Nothing but a huge collapse through all three floors.'[25] The Nazis had found the room, packed the panels into twenty-seven crates (an indication of how the room had expanded from the eighteen used to transport it in its original form) and shipped them to Königsberg Castle, in Prussia, in October 1941. There, only a part of the room was assembled and displayed. This may indicate that numerous panels were damaged, and so remained in storage, or that some were lost, discarded or stolen along the way.

That might have been the end of the story, but Königsberg was heavily bombed by the Allies in August 1944, with fires in the city centre lapping the sky for days and smouldering far longer. Adding to this devastation, the Red Army besieged the city for three months, beginning in January 1945. When surrender came, on 9 April, the castle was a ruin.[26]

The Amber Room was probably destroyed with Königsberg Castle during the bombing and the siege, but it remains possible that some panels survive – absconded with, left behind, forgotten, discarded, damaged. Indeed, one was discovered in 1997.[27] Although the room itself was not particularly influential in art historical terms – its vast expense and unique nature made it a sublime work of craftsmanship but its designer, the sculptor Andreas Schlüter, was not internationally famous – it was a powerful, quasi-legendary status symbol, an indication of the wealth of first the Prussian, and then the Russian royal families. It is perhaps fitting that a replica now stands in its place in the newly renovated Catherine Palace, opened with great pomp by Russian president Vladimir Putin in 2003.

Courbet's *The Stonebreakers*

The Amber Room may be considered collateral damage in war – its loss was not targeted, but incidental, and it happened despite efforts to preserve it. A parallel story of the Second World War is that of the treasures of the Gemäldegalerie Alte Meister in Dresden. The firebombing of the beautiful city of Dresden from 13 to 15 February 1945 is a multifaceted tragedy. The 4000 tons of incendiary bombs levelled much of the city, killing some 25,000 people and obliterating over 75,000 homes. Among the losses were 154 works from the Gemäldegalerie, a gallery that until 1945 ranked with some of the world's best museums. These included Gustave Courbet's *The Stonebreakers* (*Les Casseurs de Pierres*, 1849), which had been evacuated to a tower of Dresden Castle with other works of high value.

The Stonebreakers is one of Courbet's most important works and receives pride of place in any pantheon of lost artworks that greatly influenced cultural history. Like so many of that artist's works, its subject carries a loaded political message. The picture shows a teenage boy and an elderly man working at the side of a road, smashing and shifting rocks – a tedious, back-breaking form of manual labour. Courbet described the scene to two friends, art critics, saying, 'It is not often that one encounters

Top: Gustave Courbet, *The Stonebreakers*, 1849, oil on canvas, 165 × 257 cm (65 × 101 in), formerly the Gemäldegalerie, Dresden, destroyed 13–15 February 1945
Bottom: Jean-François Millet, *The Gleaners*, 1857, oil on canvas, 84 × 112 cm (33 × 44 in), Musée d'Orsay, Paris

so complete an expression of poverty and so, right then and there, I got the idea for a painting. I told them to come to my studio the next morning.' In terms of style, the painting would be categorized as social realism – a naturalistic image with a social message, almost a genre scene of peasant labour. One can feel the weight of the basket of stones carried by the young boy, and see his bleak future set before him, an inescapable path towards becoming, decades hence, the old man beside him. One might even imagine this as a picture of the same person, in youth and in old age, trapped within his social class. The unmistakable political charge was shocking to the patrician visitors to the 1850 Paris Salon, where the painting was first displayed. It was too real – art audiences preferred not to think about the impoverished, hopeless lot of those who toil out of sight and mind.

The work was also a departure from more idealized visions of rural peasant life. Millet's *The Gleaners* (1857) depicts similarly debilitating labour (women gathering scraps of wheat that remain in the field after a harvest), but with a sense of quiet beauty. *The Stonebreakers*, in contrast, presents poverty entirely unidealized, torturous. It is no coincidence that Courbet painted the work one year after Marx and Engels published *The Communist Manifesto* – ideas of unfair class division were very much in the air, but this is one of the first artworks to depict it with such moving rawness. The workers could be anyone, as their identity – their faces – are denied us, suggesting that we comfortable middle-class viewers would prefer not to humanize them, nor think of them at all.

The Gemäldegalerie was indeed hit by a firebomb, but so, too, was the castle tower. In addition to the 154 works that are known to have been destroyed, hundreds more were seized by Soviet soldiers as plunder and carried back to the USSR. Around 206 works have been returned to date, but an estimated 450 remain missing, presumably secreted in Russian collections.

Alexander Calder, *Bent Propeller*, 1969–70, painted metal, H: 7.62 m (25 ft), as installed at the World Trade Center, New York; destroyed on 11 September 2001

Miracles of Preservation: Composanto Monumentale, Pisa

Hope remains that part of the vast quantities of art that has disappeared in war survives (in the Second World War alone, some estimates suggest that five million cultural heritage objects changed hands inappropriately), simply because of their obvious value. The discovery of the Gurlitt hoard in 2012, with its more than a thousand artworks secreted in a single apartment, inspires a modicum of optimism that other stashes of lost treasures may surface. Objects of evident value are more likely to be preserved in any circumstances, and no one (aside from iconoclasts, who will be addressed in a later chapter) benefits when artworks are destroyed or damaged or left to decay. So perhaps some of the works now labelled as destroyed, like the Klimts from Schloss Immendorf, were spirited away? Perhaps time and circumstance will open locked doors and sealed attics, and other caches of lost art will come to light.

While art crushed and burned in a fallen building might be lost forever, like Alexander Calder's World Trade Center stabile (1969) and Joan Miró's and Josep Royo's *World Trade Center Tapestry* (1974), destroyed when the buildings collapsed on 11 September 2001 (though a portion of the Calder sculpture was recovered and is displayed in the National September 11 Memorial and Museum), others have had life breathed back into them through the remarkable efforts of conservators. The firebombing of the Second World War was not limited to Dresden, of course. The medieval monastery of Monte Cassino was pummelled by Allied bombs, for fear that Nazis were holed up in it – ironically, the enemy was not there, but they subsequently took up positions in the post-bombing rubble. The bombing of Monte Cassino is one of the most notable errors on the part of Allies who made a concerted effort, at the instruction of their Commander-in-Chief, General Dwight Eisenhower, to avoid damaging cultural heritage as much as possible. For the most part, damage at Allied hands was accidental, but that does not make it any more palatable.

On 27 July 1944, stray Allied incendiary bombs landed on the roof of the Camposanto Monumentale (Great Cemetery), part of the Field of Miracles in Pisa, adjacent to the cathedral and the famous Leaning Tower. Said to have been built on a boatload of

Buonamico Buffalmacco, *Triumph of Death*, *c.*1338–9, fresco, Composanta, Pisa; the fresco cycle – a sort of painted sermon – includes scenes called *The Three Dead and the Three Living*, and the *Triumph of Death* (shown here, from left), continuing with the *Last Judgement*, *Hell* and the *Thebais* (episodes from the lives of the Holy Fathers in the Desert)

soil taken by the Archbishop of Pisa from Calvary in Jerusalem during the Fourth Crusade, the Composanto Monumentale evolved into a Gothic cloister, one of the relatively few Gothic architectural masterpieces in Italy. Begun in 1278, when Pisa was a major cultural, economic and military power, building was put on hold in 1284, when Pisa lost the Battle of Meloria and ceded maritime power to the rival Genoans. The structure was finished in 1464, and during the fallow period in between the thirteenth and fifteenth centuries, the building was decorated with marvellous Gothic mullions, tracery and gorgeous frescoes, part of an elaborate cycle painted over the course of many decades by many different artists. These included Francesco Traini (*fl.*1321–65), Taddeo Gaddi (*c.*1290–1366), Antonio Veneziano (d.1388), Benozzo Gozzoli (*c.*1421–97)

and Buonamico Buffalmacco (*c.*1290–1340), an artist made
famous by Giorgio Vasari in his 1550 book, considered the
first work of art history, *The Lives of the Most Eminent Painters,
Sculptors and Architects*. Vasari describes Buffalmacco as
immensely talented and immensely lazy, a prankster who
would rather invest time and energy in avoiding work than
in meritorious work itself. Buffalmacco is more famous for
Vasari's entertaining portrayal of him (with memorable
anecdotes, such as his affixing lit candles to the backs of dozens
of beetles and sending them into his master's bedroom, to
make him think they were demons), than for any of his work,
almost none of which survives. His *Triumph of Death* in the
Composanto was meant to be his masterpiece, and it certainly
shows his extraordinary ability (and makes one wonder what

he might have achieved, had his personality been less inclined to pranks and more to painting).

Commissioned by Simone Saltarelli, Archbishop of Pisa from 1323 to 1342, the Composanto fresco cycle is important not only for its quality and prominence (Pisa was a destination for artists and art lovers from the thirteenth century on), but also for the collaborative nature of its creation – made over the course of two centuries by numerous artists, but with a consistent theme entirely appropriate for a cemetery: life and death. Other multi-artist fresco cycles do exist, for instance the fifteenth-century decorations of the Sistine Chapel walls, but most fresco cycles were commissioned from a single artist, produced by his studio and finished during a single generation. They were also usually the fruit of a single patron. When that patron died, or when money ran out, or when a section was completed, it marked the end of the cycle, and a new patron, with a different artist and perhaps a new theme, would start afresh elsewhere. But from 1278 through the mid-fifteenth century, a remarkable consistency of theme and even aesthetic (though artistic styles changed) makes the frescoes of the Camposanto Monumentale distinctive in the history of painting.

This appeared to have been ruined by the stray Allied bomb. It did not detonate in the cemetery itself but on a roof nearby, and a spill of molten lead from the melted rooftop smothered the frescoes. Restoration began within days, led by Yale University professor Deane Keller (1901–92), one of the so-called Monuments Men, the group of Allied officers who sought to protect and recover artworks harmed or stolen during the Second World War. While the frescoes cracked in the heat, the molten lead was gradually removed in a restoration that took place from 1945 to 2000. Much was lost: the cloister also once contained an extensive collection of Roman sculpture and sarcophagi, of which only eighty-four sarcophagi remain. But a significant portion of the frescoes was restored and can be seen today.

In thanks for his efforts, an urn containing Keller's ashes was interred in the cemetery in 2000. Occasionally, with a bit of good fortune, out of destruction, out of fire, out of ashes art can rise again.

—

On a cold, damp London street in February 2009, the queue waiting to enter Christie's Auction Rooms stretches round the block to St James's Square. The estate of the fashion designer Yves Saint-Laurent is going under the hammer, but the well-dressed crowd is not there to bid on paintings or furniture but on two bronze pieces of history: zodiac heads from the Old Summer Palace water clock, looted in 1860.

The auction made headlines thanks to the high profile of the late designer, but when it was revealed that two of the looted zodiac heads from the Summer Palace were to go under the hammer, the spotlight shone even brighter. The path of the rabbit and rat heads from Beijing to the Saint-Laurent collection is murky, though it is known that they had been purchased by an anonymous private collector at some point for a price of 14.9 million euros. When Saint-Laurent acquired them, and from whom, is unknown, but it was recognized as early as 2003 that they had been looted at the end of the Opium Wars. That year, according to Chinese state media, the government's Lost Cultural Relics Recovery Fund was offered the heads, but at a price (thought to be 20 million US dollars) it deemed 'unreasonable and unacceptable'.[28]

Rat head from the zodiac water clock at the Old Summer Palace, Beijing, before 1860, bronze, H: *c*.28 cm (11 in), National Museum of China, Beijing; the head would originally have sat atop a bronze statue with human form

Prior to the 2009 auction, Christie's stated coyly that 'In view of the public nature of an auction, the return of these works to China is not guaranteed. However, Christie's supports repatriation of cultural relics to their home country.' The auction house argued that all the items in the auction had 'clear legal title', and China was welcome to bid for the heads alongside everyone else. They did indeed go to the highest bidder, who turned out to be a Chinese national who then refused to pay, demanding that they be returned to China at no cost. Eventually, in a gesture of goodwill, François-Henry Pinault, business magnate and owner of Christie's, bought the heads and gifted them to China in 2013.[29] Seven of the twelve zodiac heads have been found and are back in Chinese museums. The rest: a snake, sheep, rooster, dog and dragon, remain lost. At least for now.

Rabbit head from the zodiac water clock at the Old Summer Palace, Beijing, before 1860, bronze, H: *c*.31 cm (12 in), National Museum of China, Beijing; as with the rat head, it would originally have topped a statue with human form

ACCIDENT

Christmas Eve in the Alcázar, 1734. Most of the occupants of the palace are at midnight mass. In a room used by court artist Jean Ranc, fire breaks out, spreading quickly along the medieval corridors and stairs. Just after midnight a guard raises the alarm. First on the scene are monks from the monastery of San Gil, but the flames are too strong now to extinguish: the fire is so hot that objects of silver and gold are melting. Hurling jewels and artworks from the windows of the Royal Chapel, the Alcázar's occupants try to save what they can, but masterpieces like Velázquez's Las Meninas *are too big and heavy to move easily, and too many are affixed to the walls. The flames draw nearer.*

By the time the fire was out, the Alcázar was a blackened shell, strewn with rubble. Begun in the ninth century, it had undergone numerous renovations and expansions, evolving from a squat stronghold (the Arabic *alcazar* means 'castle') into an elegant palace for the Habsburg rulers based in Madrid. It would be four years before a new palace rose on the site.

It is not certain exactly how many artworks burned in the conflagration, but several by Velázquez (1599–1660) were among them, including *The Expulsion of the Moriscos* (1627). The lost work was the vehicle by which Velázquez began his career. It won him a painting competition in 1627, with the prize of a post at court: Usher of the Chamber. The scene was the announcement of a decree made by Philip III (reigned 1598–1621) on 9 April 1609. The Moriscos were descendants of Muslims living in the Iberian peninsula who had been forcibly converted to Christianity during the Inquisition of the sixteenth century. Philip II (reigned 1556–98) had been concerned that they, as 'new Christians', might side with Muslim Turks who were threatening the Spanish coasts, and so between 1609 and 1614 some 300,000 (4 per cent of the total population of Spain at the time, by some accounts)[1] were expelled from the kingdom.

Other lost works include the *Equestrian Portrait of Philip IV* (1645) by Rubens (a studio of Velázquez copy of it survives), along with a 1635 Velázquez portrait of Philip IV (reigned 1621–65). Titian's *Equestrian Portrait of Charles V* (1548), which hung opposite the Rubens in the Room of Mirrors, was saved, but a series of twelve Titian paintings displayed in the Great

Room, *The Twelve Caesars* (1536), was not (only engravings of them survive), nor was Rubens' *The Rape of the Sabines* (1639) or his *Battle of the Romans* (1622). Two of Titian's four *Furies* series burned in the Room of Mirrors, while two – *Sisyphus* and *Tityus,* both 1548 – were rescued. Twenty paintings lined the walls of the Octagonal Room of the palace. Of these, gone are Tintoretto's *Pyramus and Thisbe* and *Venus and Adonis,* Veronese's *Moses in the Nile* and *Jacob,* and Jusepe de Ribera's *Jael and Sisana, Samson and Delilah, Venus and Adonis* and *Apollo and Marsyas.* Inventories list the name of artists whose works were destroyed, though not necessarily which of their paintings. At least one work by Correggio, Leonardo, Guido Reni, van Dyck, El Greco, Brueghel, Bosch, Bassano Carracci and Raphael burned, but it is not always clear which one.

Other works were rescued, including Ribera's *Martyrdom of Saint Philip, Saint Sebastian, Women in Combat, Vision of Saint Francis of Assisi* and *Penitent Magdalen.* Velázquez's *Los Borrachos, Villa Medici Landscapes, Coronation of the Virgin* and *Mercury and Argos* were saved. The last of these was one of three linked paintings; its companions, *Adonis and Venus* and *Psyche and Cupid,* were among the casualties. Fortuitously, the major part of the royal art collection, some 2,000 paintings strong, had been moved to another palace, the Buen Retiro, while construction work was underway at the Alcázar. Nevertheless, more than 500 paintings were lost in the blaze.[2]

For every work that was consumed by fire, however, there is a tale of a miniature miracle. For while the *Expulsion of the Moriscos* was among the casualties of that horrible fire, *Las Meninas,* one of the greatest paintings ever made, rose from the ashes.

—

Accidents are distinguished from natural disasters in being misfortunes brought on by human error, sometimes with nature lending a hand. Inadvertent destruction, usually through an accident that resulted in a fire or the sinking of a ship, is the most common way that large numbers of artworks have been lost in one go; ancient art in particular was frequently lost (and, as we will see, also survived) when drowned in a shipwreck.

FIRE

Major fires in which known, catalogued works were wiped out are relatively few. The Great Fire of Rome, for instance, which decimated the centre of the city under the emperor Nero in AD 64 (of fourteen city districts, three were completely levelled, and only four were largely unscathed), took unknown quantities of art with it. Because the works are not enumerated, their loss feels more generically tragic than if we knew of individual pieces we might wish had survived. To learn that 500 works were lost in the Alcázar fire is less affecting than to hear the names of specific works now gone.

One well-known conflagration was the great fire – actually, two fires – at Whitehall Palace in London at the end of the seventeenth century. The primary London residence of English kings from 1530 until 1698, larger than the Vatican or Versailles, Whitehall Palace had over 1,500 rooms and must have been more a city within a city than a traditional palace. The home of monarchs including Henry VIII, Elizabeth I, James I and Charles I, it may have been the venue for the first performance of Shakespeare's *Twelfth Night* and it certainly had ceilings painted by Rubens and buildings designed by Christopher Wren. It was a showcase for the collected artistic talent and architectural ingenuity of the English realm.

On 10 April 1694, a fire swallowed an apartment recently occupied by Louise de Kérouaille, Duchess of Portsmouth and mistress of Charles II. The blaze damaged some of the older palace buildings, but did not reach the state apartments. This was followed on 4 January 1698 by a much worse fire that gutted most of Whitehall, residential and governmental, with only Inigo Jones' Banqueting Hall intact. As diarist John Evelyn wrote the following day, with the succinct drama of a newspaper headline: 'Whitehall burnt! Nothing but walls and ruins left!' Lost were Michelangelo's *Sleeping Eros* (1496), Hans Holbein's *Portrait of Henry VIII* (1536) and Bernini's *Portrait Bust of King Charles I* (*c*.1636; in 1635, Charles had commissioned Anthony van Dyck to paint a triple portrait, showing the king from three difference angles, which Bernini used to create the sculpture so he need not leave Rome).

View of the Banqueting Hall by Inigo Jones, Whitehall, London, with ceiling fresco by Peter Paul Rubens, *c.*1628–30, *in situ*; this is the only surviving part of Whitehall Palace, destroyed by fire in 1698

A more contemporary example of the destruction of art by fire occurred on 24 May 2004 in Leyton, east London, at the Momart Storage Warehouse, a space used by numerous artists and galleries for storage of artworks and archival material. Almost all of the contents of the warehouse (with a value of some 50 million pounds sterling) were destroyed, including works owned by the collector Charles Saatchi, works by William Redgrave (whose son, Chris, salvaged thirty of 228 bronze sculptures stored there), works by Jake and Dinos Chapman, Chris Ofili, Gavin Turk, Damien Hirst, Tracey Emin and many others.

During the Alcázar fire, people were rushing back into the blaze, at the risk of their own lives, to throw canvases out the window; the names of the artworks they saved, and those they didn't, are known; their own names are not. Historians write of the Whitehall fire and record the known works by famous artists that were lost in it, but the names of people injured or killed by the fire are for the most part forgotten. Occasionally, however, the identity of a human casualty is preserved – if the name is important enough. An explosion rocked the town of Delft on 12 October 1654 when a gunpowder magazine blew up, killing a hundred people,

Tracey Emin, *Everyone I Have Ever Slept With 1963–1995*, 1995, appliquéd tent, mattress and light, 122 × 245 × 214 cm (48 × 96½ × 84¼ in), destroyed in the Momart Storage warehouse fire, 2004

Egbert Lievensz. van der Poel, *Explosion of the Powder Magazine at Delft on Monday, 12 October 1654*, 1654–60, oil on panel, 37 × 62 cm (14^1/$_2$ × 24^1/$_2$ in), Rijksmuseum, Amsterdam

wounding thousands and flattening much of the town. Thirty tons of gunpowder had been stored in a former convent, and the explosion occurred when the keeper of the magazine opened the door to check the stores. The total damage in terms of artworks is unknown, but the fire is today best remembered for having killed Carel Fabritius, Rembrandt's star pupil, and destroying almost all of his paintings.

The year after the Momart fire, the firm commissioned Jake and Dinos Chapman to design its corporate Christmas gift. The brothers produced a cigarette lighter.

SHIPWRECK

While fire almost always irreparably destroys art, water can both destroy and preserve it. We have water to thank for the salvation and preservation of countless sculptures of the ancient world. Metal artworks were all too often recycled – melted down like the bronze beams from the ceiling of the Pantheon portico, which Bernini appropriated to cast his monumental baldachino inside Saint Peter's, or like the ancient bronzes turned by the Ottoman Turks into cannonballs. But bronze sculptures that were lost at sea, taken to the bottom in shipwrecks, remained preserved – often in an excellent state. Indeed, most surviving

The Croatian *Apoxyomenos*, Roman copy after fourth-century BC original by Lysippos, first or second century AD, bronze, H: 192 cm (75¹/₂ in), Museum of Apoxyomenos, Mali Lošinj, Croatia

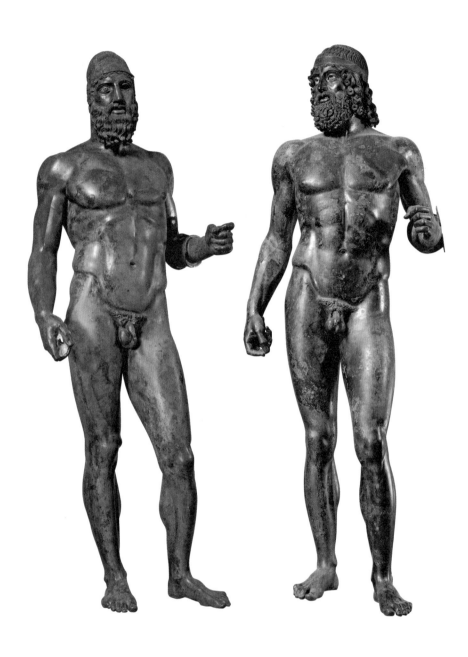

Riace Warriors, *c.*460–440 BC, bronze with copper, silver, bone and glass inlay, H: 198 cm (78 in), Museo Archeologico Nazionale di Reggio Calabria, Taranto; statue B, on the left, originally wore a helmet, and both figures would have carried a shield, spear and sword

large-scale ancient bronze sculptures have been preserved
through the good fortune of having been shipwrecked, for
example the Croation *Apoxyomenos*, discovered in 1996 near
Lošinj in the northern Adriatic; the Riace Warriors, found off
the Calabrian coast of southern Italy in 1972; the Artemision
Zeus (or Poseidon), recovered from the sea off of northern
Euboia in Greece in 1926; and others. Works of stone are also
largely unharmed by centuries or even millennia submerged
on the sea floor.

Zeus or *Poseidon*, c.460–450 BC, bronze, H: 210 cm (82½ in), Archaeological Museum, Athens

Cleopatra's Needle

A fixture of London's riverfront embankment, Cleopatra's Needle is a monumental work of stone that survives despite a shipwreck. A towering obelisk, carved with hieroglyphics, this and a companion obelisk that stands in New York City's Central Park were both carved during the reign (c.1479–1458 BC) of the female pharaoh Hatshepsut. Carved out of red granite, it weighs in at 224 tons and towers some 21 metres (69 ft) into the sky. It was first cut around 1450 BC, and some two centuries later was inscribed with scenes of the military victories of Ramesses II (reigned c.1279–1213 BC) and erected in the city of Heliopolis (now part of modern Cairo). Cleopatra VII, the last native ruler of ancient Egypt, built a new temple in Alexandria called the Caesareum, dedicated to the cult of Rome; whether it honoured Julius Caesar or Marc Antony, both of whom were Cleopatra's lovers, is uncertain, but it certainly became a centre for the

View of Cleopatra's Needle,
fifteenth century BC, granite,
H: c.21 m (69 ft), as installed
on the Embankment, London

cult of Augustus; inscriptions on the bronze crabs that once supported the two obelisks record that they were moved from Heliopolis to Alexandria around 13 BC. The placement of obelisks in front of a temple is an Egyptian architectural custom, here copied by the Roman rulers of the country.

Some 1,300 years later, the obelisks fell and were partially buried in the sands, which protected their hieroglyphic inscriptions from the battering winds of the centuries. After the Battle of Alexandria in 1801, the forces of Sir Ralph Abercromby considered raising Cleopatra's Needle to commemorate their victory over the French, and in 1819, the Egyptian ruler Pasha Mehmet Ali offered it to the United Kingdom in thanks for the defeat of Napoleon's forces by Abercromby and earlier by Admiral Lord Nelson in the 1798 Battle of the Nile. But the logistics and huge expense of transporting the gift to London kept the huge stone in the sands for another sixty years until 1877, when a wealthy dermatologist and anatomist, Sir William James Erasmus Wilson, offered the engineer John Dixon 10,000 pounds sterling

Odoardo Francisci, engraving published in *L'Illustrazione Italiana* 37 (16 September 1877), showing Cleopatra's Needle with bulkheads assembled, while fitting iron plates to create a watertight cylinder within which the obelisk would be towed from Egypt to England

to devise a way to transport it to London, to be paid only if the venture was successful.

Dixon's brother, Waynman Dixon, designed a watertight iron cylinder of enormous size, 28 metres (92 ft) long and 4.9 metres (16 ft) wide, into which the obelisk was rolled down the beach; the cylinder was fitted out with twin keels, a rudder, mast and deckhouse, and was surrounded by a floating pontoon. The whole thing was christened the *Cleopatra*, and the plan was to have it towed it to London by the steamship *Olga*.[3]

The transport ended in disaster. On 14 October 1877, a storm raged over the Bay of Biscay, and the *Cleopatra* began to roll. A dinghy sent out from the *Olga* to secure it was lost with all six crew members. The decision was taken to abandon the obelisk, and after its five-man crew was safely transferred to the *Olga*, the tow rope was released for fear of a collision between the two vessels. After the storm passed, the *Olga*'s captain searched in vain for the cylinder pontoon, but it appeared to have been lost, sunk to the bottom of the sea. The *Olga*'s despondent crew continued on without their precious cargo.

But Waynman Dixon's design kept the obelisk afloat, though unnavigable, and it was rescued and towed to the port of Ferrol

Arrival of the pontoon *Cleopatra* off of Gravesend; engraving from *The Graphic* magazine, vol. xvii, no. 427, 2 February 1878

by the steamer *Fitzmaurice*, out of Glasgow, where the captain demanded 5,000 pounds sterling as a salvage fee. (In the end, and following multiple lawsuits, John Dixon was forced to pay 9,000 pounds himself to reclaim the obelisk.) On 21 January 1878, the cylinder with its ancient cargo arrived in England; it was erected in London, at Victoria Embankment, on 12 September 1878. After a long, dangerous journey, nearly sunken, lost and rescued at sea, the three-millennia-old 'needle', as a French journalist described it, reached its final port of call.[4]

Vrouw Maria

In contrast to works nearly lost but salvaged, like Cleopatra's Needle, and the many ancient bronzes, ceramics and remains of stone statuary pulled out of the sea intact, innumerable works are still missing. The *Vrouw Maria*, a wooden Dutch merchant ship, sank off the coast of Finland on 9 October 1771. She was loaded with cargo that included cloth, coffee, sugar, dye and foodstuffs, but also the paintings *Large Herd of Oxen* (*c*.1650) by Paulus Potter and *Woman at Her Toilette* (1660) by Gerard ter Borch, as well as works by other painters of the Dutch Golden Age, such as Gerard Dou and Gabriel Metsu – all of them bought at auction for Catherine the Great of Russia. The ship had set out from Amsterdam on 5 September 1771, intending to sail to St Petersburg,[5] but a storm blew her on to rocks off the island of Jurmo, Finland. At first there was only minor damage, and for several weeks cargo was salvaged from the vessel, but waves eventually pushed the ship into deeper seas, and it began to sink despite the crew's efforts to pump out the water. It turned out that coffee beans in the cargo hold had escaped their containers and clogged the pumps.

For over two hundred years the *Vrouw Maria* lay on the sea floor, until it was rediscovered in 1999. The low salinity of the Baltic waters helped to preserve the ship and the cargo – the wooden masts, for example, are still intact. A dispute between the Finnish government (under whose auspices the treasure remains) and the Finnish team of treasure hunters who found the vessel is on-going. Divers brought six items from the deck to the surface, but the contents of the ship's cargo hold remain immersed. The holds appear to be still secure, and there is a chance that the paintings, though damaged, still physically exist and have not disintegrated. If they had been rolled and stored in watertight lead boxes, as some valuables at the time were, they might even be restorable. From 2009 to 2012, the Finnish National Board of Antiquities carried out accessibility studies on the wreck, without raising it (which would come at great cost and at the risk that exposure to oxygen would deteriorate what is now preserved). But the boxes that may contain the paintings were determined to be impossible to bring to the surface without dismantling the wreck, and the raising was deemed prohibitively expensive.[6] The project remains on hold, the state of the cargo still uncertain.

—

As the night wears on and the flames consuming the Alcázar swallow more and more irreplaceable art, Velázquez's huge painting of the young Infanta Margherita and her entourage hangs amid the smoke and heat and chaotic shouts of those trying to rescue what they can. In desperation, a man attacks the painting with a knife, cutting the canvas from its ornate frame. As the flames lick the walls, the painting is hurriedly rolled and hurled out a window. The most influential work of Spanish painting ever created is saved.

In December 2016, the American historian William B. Jordan donated a painting from his personal collection to the Prado Museum – a study by Velazquez for the face of Philip III, a detail in preparation for the lost *Expulsion of the Moriscos*.[7] This act of generosity is particularly appreciated because no one knows what Velázquez's original painting looked like; there are textual descriptions, but no known copies. When Jordan bought the work at auction in 1988, it had been misattributed to the 'circle of Justus Sustermans', a seventeenth-century Flemish painter of no great significance, and it was thought that it was a portrait of Don Rodrigo Calderon. Jordan, a specialist in Spanish art, thought it looked more like Philip III, and he may have harboured hopes that it was by Velázquez. This was confirmed

Diego Velázquez, *Portrait of Philip III*, study for the lost *The Explusion of the Moriscos* 1627, oil on canvas, 45.9 × 37 cm (18 × 14¹/₂ in), Museo del Prado, Madrid

when he brought it to the Prado for evaluation, though his assumption that it was a fragment salvaged from a larger work was incorrect; it is a stand-alone study, made in preparation for the most important of Velázquez's lost works.

Each artwork saved from the 1734 Alcázar fire is a small miracle. One can imagine the servants, monks and palace officials rushing through the blazing building, trying to save all they could: hurling works from the windows, choking on smoke, trying to decide what could be saved and what could not. One work that did survive has gone on to be considered among the most important in the history of art.

LAS MENINAS

Velázquez's 1656 self-conscious masterpiece, *Las Meninas* (*The Handmaidens*) is as much *about* painting as it is a painting. What seems to be a group portrait featuring the young Infanta Margherita was said by T. E. Lawrence to represent no less than 'the philosophy of art'.[8] The painter Luca Giordano (1634–1705) described it in 1692 as the 'theology of painting'.[9] French poet Theophile Gautier once stood in front of it and asked, 'But where is the picture?'[10] What did they mean?

The scene is Velázquez's studio in the Alcázar Palace. Pride of place goes to the Infanta Margarita, only surviving child of Philip IV and his second wife, Mariana of Austria, who appear together in the background of the composition. The Infanta is flanked by her two maids of honour (*las meninas*): Isabel de Velasco (curtsying) and Maria Augustina Sarmiento de Sotomayor. Two dwarfs are present: the stocky German Maria Barbola and the slender Italian who pokes a dog with his leg, Nicolasito Pertusato. Considered both preternaturally cunning and amusing, dwarves played important roles at the Spanish Habsburg court, as both entertainers and advisers. Behind the Infanta is her chaperone, Marcela de Ulloa, and an unidentified bodyguard. In the doorway at the back of the large studio stands a relative of Velázquez, Don José Nieto Velázquez, the Queen's chamberlain and keeper of the royal tapestries.

If you close your eyes as you look at the painting, then suddenly open them, your line of sight naturally flows to the work's perspectival vanishing point – in this case, the open doorway at the back of the painting. Velázquez himself stands before a canvas so large that it must be the very canvas of *Las Meninas* at which we are looking.

The painting is full of unsolved mysteries. To begin with, Velázquez himself appears, paintbrush and palette in hand. It was radical at the time to represent an artist in the process of portraying other, far more important, individuals. And then the myriad other figures, all identifiable members of court – what is the significance of their presence in a portrait of the princess? There is more. At the back of the room, either in a framed painting or framed mirror, stand the king and queen. The bevelled edges whisper to us that it is a mirror, but what does it reflect? Do we see the real king and queen, or a portrait of them that Velazquez is painting on the canvas before him? Since all attention is directed towards the front of the canvas, where the viewer stands, one theory suggests that Philip and his queen are physically present in the room with those portrayed, their reflections seen in the mirror at the back of the room.[11]

But why does Velázquez look directly at us? There is an artistic tradition that the artist does not look directly at the subject of a portrait while painting, but rather looks at the sitter in a mirror. This is most obvious when one paints a self-portrait: one must look in a mirror to see oneself. Artists also usefully used the technique to portray others, though. It puts the subject inside a frame, that of the mirror itself, so that the painter can more easily compose the picture, and it transfers the three-dimensional subject on to the two-dimensional surface of the mirror. This depiction of three dimensions on to a two-dimensional surface is the essential act of painting.

Diego Velázquez, *Las Meninas*, 1656, oil on canvas, 108 × 81 cm (42^1/$_2$ × 31^3/$_4$ in), Museo del Prado, Madrid

In terms of this technique then, where is the mirror? *We* are the mirror. The front of the painting at which we, the viewers, stare is in fact a mirror, bouncing the scene trapped inside the painting back to Velázquez's eyes. As with a pane of one-way glass, we can see through it, while Velázquez and those within the painting see only their own reflections in it. But by staring at their reflections, they make eye contact with us, on the far side of the one-way glass. They break the fourth wall, to borrow the theatrical term, announcing to us that they are aware of themselves as figures inside a work of art, and that they know we are staring in at them. In a complex reading of the work by Michel Foucault in *The Order of Things* (1966), the philosopher wrote that Velázquez crafted a work self-conscious of itself as an artwork, a painting about the act of painting – the first post-modernist work of art.

Saved from the Alcázar Palace fire in 1734, *Las Meninas* was nevertheless damaged: the painting had to be cut down at the edges and parts of it repainted, including all of the Infanta's left cheek. Painted four years before his death, Velázquez intended this to be his masterwork, the means to achieve his dream of a knighthood, which he finally received mere months before his death. (Knighthood required the approval of a royal commission, which had found questionable elements in Velázquez's heritage, perhaps Jewish or Muslim blood, thus delaying the king's ability to grant the honour that his court painter so desired.) After receiving his knighthood, Velázquez revisited *Las Meninas*, adding to his garment in the painting the emblem of his new title, the red cross of the Order of Santiago. An unsubstantiated romantic version of the addition of the cross relates that King Philip IV painted it himself after Velázquez's death, to record the honour of his friend for posterity.[12]

ICONOCLASM
& VANDALISM

*In the lavish Papal apartments of the Vatican, Clement VII
sweats uncomfortably into his velvet robes. The autumn of 1524
is hot, even for Rome, and the engravings on the table in front
of him are raising the temperature more. He studies each in
turn, sixteen in all, then with a snort of disgust sweeps them to
the floor. 'Find every copy and burn them', he says. 'Every one!
And make sure Marcantonio is in prison before the sun rises
tomorrow.' Gian Matteo Giberti stoops to pick up the scattered
pages. 'Leave them! Go!'*

Marcantonio Raimondi (d.1534) was among the most famous
and skilful engravers of the sixteenth century. He was a major
artist in his own right, but he was best known for having been
Raphael's official printmaker, creating exquisite engravings based
on that artist's paintings. The engraving technique involves
incising a metal (usually copper) plate with a burin. The plate
is inked and then wiped clean, leaving ink in the incisions.
Moist paper is pressed on the plate and into the engraved lines,
producing a mirror image on the paper. The printing technique
allowed for an infinite number of reproductions to be made; sold
for a reasonable cost, they were disseminated throughout Europe
and were the means by which Raphael achieved international
renown, even among people who had never seen his paintings.

But Raimondi also had a naughty streak. He was the subject
of one of the first intellectual property lawsuits in history,
a case brought in Venice in 1506 by Albrecht Dürer.[1] Dürer,
Europe's most famous printmaker, spotted nearly exact forgeries
of some of his works being sold from the Dal Jesus print shop
in Venice. Raimondi had even included Dürer's trademark,
a large letter A with a smaller letter D between the legs of the
A, which was seen as a guarantee that the work was Dürer's.
But wily Raimondi had also included three difficult-to-spot
differences in his prints that made them not *exact* copies of
Dürer's – his own small monogram, the device of the Dal Jesus
publishing house, and an anagram of Christ – and so was able
to claim that his prints were not forgeries but were merely
done in homage to the master artist. In the end, the Venetian
judges forced Raimondi to remove Dürer's monogram, and the
Dal Jesus firm was required to sell the prints as copies, not as

originals; the victory was Dürer's, but the outcome was not a resounding success.

Raimondi also created the images for an early work of printed pornography called *I Modi* (*The Positions*), also known as *The Sixteen Pleasures* (*De omnibus Veneris Schematibus, 'Concerning All the Figures of Love'*). The sixteen explicit engravings of sexual positions were based on a lost series of paintings by Giulio Romano (1499–1546), Raphael's pupil; they had been painted for Federico II Gonzaga, to decorate and provide inspiration at his Palazzo Te in Mantua (destroyed in 1630). Raimondi first published the engravings in 1524, and despite his worldliness, the Medici Pope Clement VII was unimpressed and threw him into prison, ordering all copies of the engravings burned. Interestingly, Giulio Romano was not punished for his original paintings, because they were never intended for public viewing, being made purely for the private enjoyment of the duke of Mantua.

—

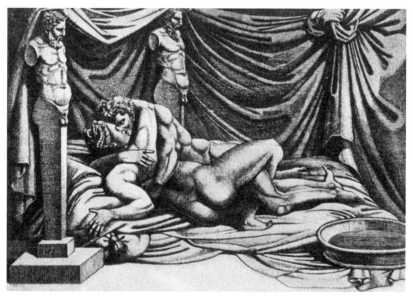

Copy after a lost print by Marcantonio Raimondi, from *I Modi*, 1524; this copper engraving was made to illustrate Sonnet 1 in Pietro Aretino's *Sonetti Lussuriosi* ('Lascivious Sonnets'), published in 1527

The distinction between vandalism and iconoclasm is one of symbolism and intent. Iconoclasm (from the Greek *eikon*, meaning 'image') comes into play when the target is selected because of what it represents. Terrorists flew airplanes into the World Trade Center towers in New York City and into the Pentagon building in Washington, DC, in acts of iconoclasm. These buildings represented, among other things, capitalism and Western society, to which the terrorists were opposed. The buildings themselves did nothing objectionable – it was what they represented (or, in this case, what people did while inside them). Vandalism, on the other hand, refers to defacing, mutilating or destroying objects or buildings with no symbolic weight given to the choice of target.

VANDALISM

Vandalism, when it targets art, is an instance of aggressive foolishness, rather than malice aforethought. These are passionless attacks, fuelled not by hate or a determination to exterminate what the target represents. The stories of vandalism of art can seem silly and often random.

Victim: the Fountain of Neptune, Florence

The Fountain of Neptune, sculpted in 1565 by Bartolomeo Ammannati (1511–92), stands prominently in Florence's main square, Piazza della Signoria. It was built to commemorate the wedding of Francesco de' Medici to Joanna of Austria in December of that year. The main statue of the fountain, representing Neptune (Poseidon), god of the sea, was nicknamed *Biancone*, 'the big white one', by sixteenth-century critics, and Giorgio Vasari, in his 1568 edition of *Lives of the Most Eminent Painters, Sculptors and Architects*, said that Michelangelo, eighty-seven years old at the time, was unimpressed by the sculpture, which stood beside his *David* in front of the Palazzo Vecchio. He is said to have murmured, 'Ammannati, what a beautiful piece of marble you have ruined!'[2] The fountain was damaged on numerous occasions, sometimes wilfully, other times not. Locals would bring their laundry to the fountain for washing, and this

Bartolomeo Ammannati, Neptune Fountain, 1565, marble, H: *c*.5.6 m (18 ft; central sculpture), Piazza della Signoria, Florence

casual, practical use may have caused early wear and tear. It was enough of a problem that a bronze plaque, still visible today, was posted beside the fountain: 'Around this fountain measuring twenty ells let nobody dare to leave any kind of rubbish, wash in it inkpots, clothes or any other thing, nor throw in wood or other rubbish, under penalty of four ducats and the judgement of their Lordships.' The fountain was vandalized and parts of it were stolen on 25 January 1580, and the diarist Agostino Lapini wrote in 1596 that 'the beautiful fountain in Piazza del Duca was damaged, and of all the decorations only the four bronze figures and their satyrs remained.'[3] During Carnival in February 1830, thieves stole a bronze satyr from the fountain; it was later replaced with a version sculpted by Giovanni Pazzi.

The most recent act of vandalism occured on 4 August 2005, when three students decided to take photographs of themselves sitting on the Neptune statue. In their attempt to climb it they broke off the god's right hand and a portion of his trident. They were caught when their escapade was filmed by CCTV cameras. The statue underwent restoration in 2007, only for four

Michelangelo Buonarroti, *David*, 1501–4, marble, H: 4.3 m (14 ft), Galleria della Accademia, Florence; the left foot was attacked, breaking off part of the big toe

teenagers to try to vandalize it once more that same year. This time it was under careful watch, though, and police intervened before it was damaged.

Vandal: Piero Cannata

While these incidents of vandalism could be dismissed as harmful idiocy, vandals occasionally target art with great determination, not for normal anti-social reasons but as a result of psychosis. While the Italian vandal Piero Cannata has not yet been responsible for the complete loss of any artwork, it is not for lack of effort. In 1991, Cannata smuggled a hammer into the Galleria della Accademia in Florence and used it to smash the toes of Michelangelo's *David* (1501–4) before he was tackled by museum visitors who kept him pinned down until the police arrived.[4] When asked why he did it, Cannata claimed that a Veronese painting had told him to. Cannata was judged mentally ill after a trial and was hospitalized, but he continued to attack artworks after his release.[5]

In 1993, he was arrested by the Carabinieri, Italy's military police, after he defaced a fifteenth-century fresco by Filippo Lippi at Prato Cathedral, and that same year he knifed another painting in Prato, *Adoration of the Shepherds Before Baby Jesus* by the sixteenth-century artist Michele di Raffaello della Colombe. He explained his actions by saying simply that 'a force inside me compelled me to do it.'

He was at it again in 1999, when he took a felt-tip pen to Jackson Pollock's 1947 *Undulating Paths* at the Galleria Nazionale d'Arte Moderna in Rome. When arrested, prior to another spell at a psychiatric hospital, he claimed to have been looking for a work by Italian painter Piero Manzoni (1933–63), but unable to locate one, he 'found an equally ugly one and damaged it instead'.[6]

Whatever psychiatric therapy Cannata was getting during his hospital stays was not working. In 2005, he spray-painted a black X on the bronze plaque at the centre of Piazza della Signoria in Florence, a few paces from the Neptune Fountain; it marks the spot where Girolamo Savonarola (see below) was burned. There is a poetic irony to this act that was almost certainly lost on Cannata: that he should attack a plaque commemorating

the destruction of a man on the spot on which that terrible
iconoclast had destroyed so much art.

ICONOCLASM

Vandalism is an act of delinquency that is not worth studying
from the perspective of the target defaced; the psychology
of the vandal may be of interest, but the object chosen for
victimization is usually irrelevant. Iconoclasm, on the other
hand, bears scrutiny in terms of both the attacker and the
'victim'. Iconoclasm in the name of religious or political
ideology, four examples of which are described below, or in the
name of moral decency, as reflected in the fate of Marcantonio
Raimondi's *I Modi* engravings, both reflect a belief that the
target exhibits attributes unacceptable to the attacker.

Hagia Sophia
Iconoclasm under the Eastern Roman, or Byzantine, empire
(330–1453) gave the term its original definition, based on two
Greek words meaning 'image' (*eikon*) and 'break, destroy' (from
klan). A ban on religious images as idolatrous (in keeping with
a literal interpretation of the second of the Ten Commandments)
was first instituted under the emperor Leo III (reigned
AD 717–41) around 726 and continued until 787; during this
period, existing images in churches – figural mosaics, frescoes
and icons – were painted over or destroyed. There was a lull
between AD 787 and 813, when the iconodules ('image servers')
gained the upper hand, but iconoclasm was firmly reinstituted
under Leo V (reigned AD 813–20). It was a tumultuous time,
and the debate, sometimes violent, was entirely Christian.
Interestingly, both periods of iconoclasm ended when a female
leader rose to power. Empress Irene reigned in her own right
from 797 to 802 but was highly influential from 775 as Empress
consort, dowager and regent. Empress Theodora, wife of
Theophilos (reigned AD 829–42) was an iconophile ('image
lover') who served as regent for her son Michael III (reigned
AD 842–67) during the first thirteen years of his rule. She had
the iconoclastic Patriarch of Constantinople deposed in 843 and
replaced with one sympathetic to the veneration of icons. From

Haïia Sophia - Constantinople

then on, images of the members of the Holy Family and saints remained a vital part of Byzantine, and subsequently Orthodox Christian, religion.

Hagia Sophia ('Holy Wisdom') and was built in only five years (AD 532–35) under the emperor Justinian I (reigned AD 527–65). The Great Church was originally decorated with non-figural decoration, and the breathtakingly beautiful gold mosaics that today sparkle and shine in the ancient building were mostly installed between AD 843, at the end of the second period of iconoclasm, and the fall of Constantinople to the Catholic armies of the Fourth Crusade in 1204, when soldiers looted much of the city's art.

Almost exactly 250 years later, in 1453, the Byzantine Empire finally fell to the Muslim forces of Sultan Mehmet II (reigned 1444–46 and 1451–81), who made the city the centre of his Ottoman Empire. When a new faction comes to power in a territory occupied by a culture with a different belief system, iconoclasm often follows, and such was the case in the former Byzantium. The Ottoman conquerors converted the Great Church of Hagia Sofia into a mosque, in which guise many of its irreplaceable mosaic decorations were not destroyed but hidden. The vast walls and domes and vaults were plastered over and whitewashed, their idolatrous mosaics protected, ironically, until attitudes changed again.

In 1847 a pair of Swiss-Italian brothers, Gaspare and Giuseppe Fossati, were appointed by the Ottoman Sultan Abdülmecid I to oversee the restoration of Hagia Sophia. Over the course of two years their army of workers cleaned away paint and plaster to reveal mosaics that had not been seen for nearly four centuries. The mosaics were recorded in drawings, but the complete restoration would have to wait until 1931, when the project was undertaken by the American scholar and Byzantinist Thomas Whittemore. Sadly, many of the mosaics documented by the Fossati brothers were no longer to be found. An earthquake in 1894 had taken its toll, and other fragments may have fallen prey to looters and treasure hunters. Upon the completion of the

Top: Roger Hayward, *Hajia Sofia*, 1926, pencil and watercolour on paper, 17.8 × 25.4 cm (7 × 10 in), Oregan State Libraries, Corvallis, Oregon
Bottom: Hagia Sophia, Istanbul, view of interior

Mother of God and Christ Child, mid-ninth century AD, mosaic, H: *c.*4 m (13 ft),
Hagia Sophia, Istanbul

conservation project in 1934, Turkish President Mustafa Kemal Ataturk officially proclaimed Hagia Sophia a museum.

Girolamo Savonarola and the Bonfire of the Vanities

The Dominican friar Girolamo Savonarola (d.1498) was one of the greatest villains in the history of art. The monk from Ferrara, resident at the monastery of San Marco in Florence, was by all accounts a hugely charismatic public speaker, and he rose in prominence during the Florentine High Renaissance as he preached against corruption in the Catholic Church, exploitation of the poor, and what he saw as the immorality of secular art and culture. He announced prophecies and then interpreted their fulfilment, publishing in 1495 a compendium of how his predictions had come true and winning legions of followers in the city. He foresaw a 'biblical flood', for instance, and a 'new Cyrus from the north' who would reform the Church, a prophecy that seemed foretold when Charles VIII of France invaded Italy in September 1494. It was a time of intense dissatisfaction with the ruling Medici, who were forcibly expelled from Florence that year. Savonarola was installed as leader of the Florentine Republic, which he proclaimed a 'New Jerusalem', a new world centre for Christianity (thus usurping Rome).

Unsurprisingly, Pope Alexander VI (reigned 1492–1503) was not amused, particularly when a Savonarola-led Florence refused to join his Holy League against the French threat. Savonarola was summoned to Rome but refused to go. He was banned from preaching but did so anyway. Finally, in May 1497, Alexander excommunicated the monk. In April 1498 a rival Florentine preacher demanded Savonarola undergo a trial by fire, to prove that he really was chosen by God; if he could walk, unharmed, through a bonfire, it would show that he truly was what he claimed. When he demurred, public opinion quickly shifted against him. Savonarola was arrested and forced to confess to having invented his prophecies. On 23 May 1498, he was hanged, and his body was burned in Piazza della Signoria.[7]

The spot on which Savonarola's body was cremated, which was marked by the plaque that Cannata defaced, is of particular, heartbreaking interest to art lovers. For part of Savonarola's legacy was his determination to destroy any art that did not conform to his own puritanical religious standards. He encouraged gangs to roam Florence, even breaking into private homes to drag out any artworks with subject matter not considered sufficiently sober and religious. Along with hundreds of paintings and sculptures, perhaps more, objects associated with personal vanity and frivolity were also condemned: everything from mirrors to dice to books to playing cards to fashionable clothing. Great piles of these 'vanities' were burned in enormous bonfires, the largest occurring on 7 February 1497, at the exact spot in Piazza della Signoria where Savonarola himself would be burned one year later.

Savonarola was such a compelling speaker that he even managed to convince one of the finest artists in Florence to destroy his own works. Giorgio Vasari describes Sandro Botticelli (1445–1510), impassioned by the preacher's rhetoric, carrying some of his own paintings to the square to be burned. Botticelli's world-famous *Primavera* (*c*.1482) and *The Birth of Venus* (*c*.1484) both survived only because they were held at the Villa di Castello, a Medici country residence outside of Florence and beyond the reach of both Savonarola's minions and Botticelli himself.

Top: Sandro Botticelli, *Primavera*, c.1482, grease tempera on panel, 203 × 314 cm
(6 ft 8 in × 10 ft 3¹/₂ in), Galleria degli Uffizi, Florence
Bottom: Sandro Botticelli, *The Birth of Venus*, c.1484, tempera on canvas, 172.5 × 278.5 cm
(5 ft 8 in × 9 ft 1¹/₂ in), Galleria degli Uffizi, Florence

Top: Adolf Hitler touring the Degenerate Art ('Entartete Kunst') exhibition, Munich, 1937
Bottom: Otto Dix, *War Cripples (45% Fit for Service)*, 1920, oil on canvas, destroyed

The Degenerate Art Exhibition

Savonarola's fifteenth-century bonfires were mirrored by Nazi book burnings and bonfires of art in the 1930s; the biggest conflagration took place on 10 May 1933. Prior to the Second World War, the German government implemented a policy in which art deemed 'degenerate' (encompassing most modern, abstract or minimalist art by any artist, as well as art created by minorities, Jews and other undesirables) could be seized by the State. This material was the subject of a travelling exhibition in 1937, curated to make the art in it look as unappealing as possible, with the message on the gallery wall: 'It is from this that the Nazis have saved your children'.[8] It was held the same year as the Great German Art Exhibition, in which approved works were featured. After the hugely popular Degenerate Art exhibition closed, in an act of utter hypocrisy, the Nazi government held auctions, selling off the despised works. Unlike Savonarola, who could not countenance the existence of works of which he disapproved, the Nazis knew that there were profits to be had and a war effort to be funded. At the Galerie Fischer, in Lucerne, Switzerland, scores of 'degenerate' works were sold to the highest bidder, including British and American collectors who could not resist the chance to acquire such trophies. The works that did not sell at auction were burned. It is assumed that this was the fate of Otto Dix's 1920 *War Cripples*, which featured in the Degenerate Art exhibition and has not been seen since; it survives only in a photograph and a drypoint etching.

ISIS: The Hypocrisy of Iconoclasm

While the Muslim conquerors of Constantinople merely hid under whitewash what they considered idolatrous in the church of Hagia Sophia, today's Islamic fundamentalists go further, attempting to destroy any art and architecture contrary to their creed – unless it can be sold to raise funds for their cause.

In the fight against Islamic State (ISIS) terrorists and their theft and destruction of art, specifically in reaction to the horrifying destruction of statues in Mosul Museum and the bulldozing of the ancient city of Nimrud, both in Iraq, two important developments occurred in 2015. First, Ahmed Al-Tayeb, grand imam of the Egyptian Islamic Institute

Al-Azhar, the oldest university in the world, issued a *fatwa* forbidding the destruction of ancient artefacts.[9] The term *fatwa* describes a learned interpretation of Islamic religious law in the form of a decree, a spiritual parallel to a Supreme Court ruling interpreting the US Constitution. This decree from the foremost authority of Sunni Islam declared, 'These artefacts have important cultural and historical significance. They are an important part of our collective legacy that must not be harmed.' The statement went on to point out ISIS's hypocrisy, on the one hand selling ancient artefacts for enormous profit, on the other destroying them on principle as non-Islamic 'idols'. In relation to that hypocrisy, the United Nations Security Council unanimously passed Resolution 2199, which condemned ISIS, al-Qaeda and other terrorist groups for using 'the looting and smuggling of cultural heritage [as a means to fund] recruitment efforts and strengthen their operational capability to organize and carry out terrorist attacks.'[10] This was quickly followed by an announcement from the Financial Action Task Force of the G-7 (the seven most economically advanced countries) stating that ISIS may 'have earned as much as tens of millions' of dollars by selling antiquities looted from Syrian territory alone.[11]

As early as 2005, US Marine Colonel Matthew Bogdanos and his colleagues presented evidence at the annual Interpol conference in Lyon on stolen works of art, showing that terrorist groups were funding their activities by selling looted antiquities abroad.[12] That same year, an article in the German periodical *Der Spiegel* revealed that Mohammed Atta, one of the al-Qaeda organizers of the 9/11 attacks on New York's World Trade Center, had flown to Germany in 1999 with Polaroids of looted Afghan antiquities, seeking advice in selling them.[13] When asked why he wanted to sell them, he replied that he wished to buy a plane. It seems that an earlier plan for the 2001 attacks using commercial airliners would have seen airplanes purchased through funds raised by selling looted antiquities, in order to crash them into American buildings. Makers of a 2009 Belgian documentary, *Blood Antiques*, filmed undercover to demonstrate how the Taliban had taken over antiquities looting from local peasant tomb raiders, using bulldozers to open tombs, destroying them in the process of gathering saleable antiquities.[14] The smuggling routes for these antiquities were largely by plane via Pakistan and then to Brussels, where art dealers were caught on camera explaining how to pass these looted objects off as legitimate, in order to sell them for maximum price on the open market.

ISIS's videos of human executions and the destruction of artworks and monuments are the latest chapter in the story of art and terrorism. The organization accepts the value of antiquities but also destroys them, an illogical hypocrisy reminiscent of Nazi theories on 'degenerate' art. The art the Nazi high command disliked was to be destroyed – unless they could profit from it. In the same way, those of 'lesser races' were not killed outright but were used as an economic commodity, as long as they could work and be reasonably sustained. It is easy to pair ISIS and the Nazis: the former obsessed with a warped interpretation of a real religion, the latter having cobbled together their own pseudo-spiritual amalgam of Aryan supremacist beliefs.

ISIS's obliteration of the ancient Assyrian city of Nimrud echoes the destruction by the Afghan Taliban of the monumental standing Buddha statues at Bamiyan, dynamited in 2001.

Bamiyan valley, Hazarajat, Afghanistan, showing the empty niche of the larger of two fourth- to fifth-century AD standing Buddhas after destruction by the Taliban, March 2001

Gateway in the palace of Ashurnasirpal II, Assyrian king of Nimrud, 884–859 BC, before destruction by ISIS forces; the *lamassu* is an apotropaic deity usually shown with the body of a lion or ox, wings and a human head

Nimrud thrived for six centuries after its construction by King Shalmaneser I around 1250 BC, at the crook of the Tigris and Great Zab rivers, in the heart of Mesopotamia. It was huge in ancient terms, expanding to some 360 hectares (890 acres), and is mentioned in the Bible (Genesis 10) as the city of Calah.[15] Ashurnasirpal II made Nimrud his capital in the ninth century BC, and most of the buildings that could be seen as excavated ruins prior to ISIS's intervention date to this period. The city supported an astonishing 100,000 inhabitants and featured not only palaces and temples, but also a zoo and a botanical garden. Little more than a century later, however, Sargon II moved the capital to Dur Sharrukin, and decline set in. By the end of the seventh century BC, waves of invaders – Babylonians, Scythians and Persians, to name but a few – had slashed away at the dying Assyrian Empire, and Nimrud fell into ruin. Among its most notable remnants were the *lamassu*, colossal statues of mythical creatures with the head of a bearded man, wings, and the torso and legs of a lion, set as guardians of entryways. It was one of these *lamassu*, still *in situ*, that ISIS videoed themselves destroying. The site was first properly excavated in 1845–7 and in 1949–51 by Austen Henry Layard, and most of the artefacts

Photograph of Nimrud after destruction by ISIS forces, November 2016

James Fergusson, *The Palaces at Nimrud Restored*, in Austin Henry Layard, *A Second Series of the Monuments of Nineveh* (London: John Murray, 1853), plate 1; the painting imagines the buildings of Nimrud and the palace of Ashurnasirpal II in the ninth century BC

Colonna Venus, Roman copy of fourth-century BC *Aphrodite of Knidos* by Praxiteles, first or second century AD, marble, H: 204 cm (80¹/₄ in), Museo Pio-Clementino, Musei Vaticani, Rome

and moveable monuments found were moved to museums, fortunately keeping them out of iconoclastic hands. In January 2017, after ISIS was driven out of Nimrud, the extent of the damage they had inflicted was clear. The site was completely in ruins but, as one of the locals said, with a sigh of optimism, 'The good thing is, the rubble is still *in situ*. The site is restorable.'[16]

—

London, 1972. The curator in the Prints and Drawings Department of the British Museum inserts an acquisition card into his typewriter and turns to peer closely at the sheet of heavy paper on which are mounted nine engravings. It is clear that these are fragments cut from larger images, apparently to excise any explicit details. Still, they are all that remain of Marcantonio Raimondi's original engravings, so successfully suppressed by the Medici Pope. It will be argued later that these are themselves copies, and that Clement VII had indeed managed to destroy the entire issue of Raimondi's Positions. But for now, the curator types the date, 1524, on the card.

The earliest story of sexually stimulating art concerns the lost statue we call the Aphrodite of Knidos, carved by the sculptor Praxiteles in the fourth century BC. Tradition says that Praxiteles was commissioned by the islanders of Kos to create a cult statue for their temple. He carved two Aphrodites, one draped and one completely nude. The citizens of Kos were shocked and refused the nude statue, which was then installed in the temple of Aphrodite at Knidos, on the south-east coast of modern Turkey. It was famous for being the first fully nude female sculpture in Classical Greek art, and was so life-like that it was sexually arousing. Indeed, one night a young man is said to have broken into the temple and tried to engage in intercourse with it, leaving a stain on the marble thighs.

However arousing, though, Praxiteles' sculpture was a religious work of art. Raimondi's beautiful engravings, on the other hand, were intended to be widely distributed and might thus be seen as qualifying for the title 'pornography'. (It turned out that Guilio Romano had no idea the engravings existed, and was only informed when visited by one of the great personalities of the Italian Renaissance, another man with a wonderfully naughty streak, Pietro Aretino (1492–1556)).

The best friend of the painter Titian, Aretino hosted raucous parties at his palazzo in Venice and was known as a great wit, referred to as the 'scourge of princes' for his scathing repartee. To get a sense of him, you need only learn how he died: the story goes that he had a stroke induced by laughing too hard at a dirty joke made at the expense of his sister.

Aretino wrote plays and sonnets and particularly liked Raimondi's style of art; he decided to compose sixteen sexually explicit sonnets (the *Sonetti Lussuriosi*, 'Lascivious Sonnets') to accompany the *I Modi* engravings. He negotiated Raimondi's release from prison, and a second edition of the prints, now with Aretino's text, was published in 1527. This was the first time

Page from Pietro Aretino, *Sonetti Lussuriosi* ('Lascivious Sonnets', 1527), written to accompany Marcantonio Raimondi's *I Modi*, engravings after Guilio Romano

that erotic text and images were combined, and the first time pornographic images (which happened to be very beautiful and by a great artist) were mass-produced. Pope Clement VII was still unimpressed, and attempted to destroy all copies of this edition, too; some scholars believe that the fragments in the British Museum are all that remains of this this later copy, and that the original Raimondi edition was completely destroyed.[17] The papal dragnet turned out to have holes, however (perhaps because the pope had other things on his mind in 1527, such as the sacking of Rome by the renegade army of Charles V). A pirated, rather crudely copied edition was printed in Venice circa 1550; black market pornography had a market even in the sixteenth century. The painter and printmaker Agostino Carracci (1557–1602) arranged for a reprinting of Aretino's poems in the 1580s and seems to have copied the original engravings, some of which must have survived.[18] Two seventeenth-century fellows

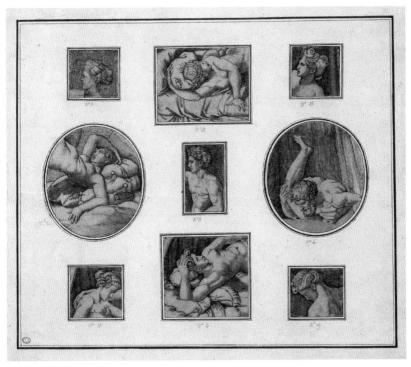

Marcantonio Raimondi, *I Modi*, after Giulio Romano, *c*.1524, engraving on paper, 24 × 27 cm (9^1/$_2$ × 10^1/$_2$ in), British Museum, London; nine fragments of larger images, now lost

Annibale Carracci, *Triumph of Bacchus and Ariadne*, c.1597–1600, fresco, from the series *Loves of the Gods*; central panel, detail of the Gallery ceiling, L (gallery): 20.2 m (66 ft), Palazzo Farnese, Rome

at All Souls College, Oxford, oversaw the printing of an English edition at Oxford University Press, entitled *Aretino's Postures*; the dean at the time confiscated the copper plates used for the engravings.[19]

Agostino Carracci's interest in *I Modi* (whether artistic or corporeal or both) resulted in an adaptation of its poses for the Carracci frescoes at the Farnese Gallery, and so had a lasting influence on the history of art. The great hall at the Palazzo Farnese in Rome was painted by Annibale Carracci (1560–1609) and his studio; Annibale, his brother Agostino and their cousin Ludovico were the leading academic painters of the seventeenth century (the Carracci also ran a painting academy in Bologna). The ceiling of that room (now part of the French Embassy in Rome) is decorated with astounding paintings on the theme of gods seducing mortals, making plastic the popular ancient Latin poetry of Ovid's *Metamorphoses*. Annibale Carracci's *Loves of the Gods* is a degree less risqué than the images in *I Modi*, and lost though those pornographic engravings may be, the artistic influence of Raimondi's prints is unmistakable.

ACTS OF GOD

*In the early afternoon, my mother drew his attention to a cloud
of unusual size and appearance. Its general appearance can
be best expressed as being like an umbrella pine, for it rose to a
great height on a sort of trunk, and then split off into branches.
I imagine, because it was thrust upwards by the first blast,
and then left unsupported as the pressure subsided, or else
it was borne down by its own weight, so that it spread out and
gradually dispersed. Sometimes it looked white, sometimes
blotched and dirty, according to the amount of soil and ashes
it carried with it.*

So wrote Pliny the Younger to the historian Tacitus, describing
the events he witnessed on 24 August AD 79.[1] On that day the
volcano called Mount Vesuvius began a two-day eruption.
There had been warnings: a major earthquake in AD 62 was not
recognized as a danger sign, nor was the smaller quake that
followed two years later.[2] Seneca the Younger wrote of sheep
dying from 'tainted air' following the first quake, which modern
volcanologists have linked to carbon dioxide emissions from the
volcano: 'they say that a flock of hundreds of sheep was killed,
statues cracked, and some people were deranged and afterwards
wandered about unable to help themselves'.[3] Nevertheless,
this was not the sort of thing that would prompt evacuation of
a city with a population of around 15,000, when there had been
no eruption in known history.[4] Pliny acknowledged that such
earthquakes were 'not particularly alarming because they are

Pierre-Jacques Volaire, *Eruption of Vesuvius*, 1771, oil on canvas, 116.8 × 242.9 cm
(46 × 95^1/$_2$ in), Art Institute of Chicago

frequent'. On this day in August, Pliny was visiting his uncle, the writer and philosopher Pliny the Elder, at his house in Misenum, across the Bay of Naples from Pompeii – far enough away to be safe, but close enough to see an explosion that has been described as having a thermal energy 10,000 times greater than that of the atomic bomb dropped on Hiroshima.[5] From his position across the bay, Pliny could see the geyser of gas, ash and rock that shot 33 kilometres (21 miles) into the sky, spewing out lava and ash at a rate of around 1.5 million tons per second. The population would have been killed primarily by suffocation from the noxious gases that billowed out of the collapsing volcano, and they were then buried by the showers of ash, which later hardened around them.[6] In addition to people and animals, the eruption smothered whole towns worth of art – uncounted paintings, frescoes, sculptures, items of jewellery, coins and other artworks, buried beneath metres of ash and pumice, lost for eighteen centuries.

—

EARTHQUAKE:
SHATTERING THE WONDERS OF THE WORLD

While the hand of man, through intent or accident, has been responsible for most of the art lost to history, there are numerous cases in which no person can be blamed. Nature, time, what some might call 'acts of God', have robbed us of countless treasures. Volcanic eruptions are, fortunately, rare; in contrast, one of the most frequent culprits, particularly in the ancient world, was earthquake.

The Colossus of Rhodes

Among the Seven Wonders of the Ancient World was a colossal bronze statue, apparently about a third of the height of New York's Statue of Liberty (33 metres, 108 ft). Portraying the sun god, Helios, it stood at the entrance to what was called the Mandraki harbour on the island of Rhodes (not straddling it, as is a common misconception)[7]. The statue was made to commemorate the victorious resistance of the people of Rhodes against a siege by Antigonus I Monophthalmus, ruler of Macedon, in 305 BC. King Ptolemy of Egypt sent an armada to Rhodes,

Sidney Barclay, *The Colossus of Rhodes*, nineteenth century, in Lucian Augé de Lassus, *Voyage to the Seven Wonders of the World* (1878); engraving showing the Colossus of Rhodes as it probably stood, beside the entrance to the harbour of the city

Engraving after original by Marten Jacobsz. Heemskerk van Veen, sixteenth century, showing the more conventional, but probably incorrect position of the Colossus of Rhodes, astride the harbour entrance

routing the Macedonians in 304 BC. The statue, begun in 292 BC and completed in 280 BC, was designed by Chares of Lindos (a pupil of the famous fourth-century BC Rhodian sculptor Lysippos) and would have been built by an extensive workshop in a pointed act of recycling. The Macedonian army had been forced to surrender, abandoning vast quantities of arms and siege machinery (including what is considered the first moveable siege tower, called a *helepolis*). Pliny the Elder wrote in the first century AD that the people of Rhodes sold the siege equipment for 300 silver talents and melted down the weapons and the bronze carapace of the *helepolis* to provide the materials and funds to build their war memorial.

Early sources, including Pliny the Elder and the third-century BC engineer Philo of Byzantium, describe the Colossus as having been constructed from iron tie bars to which a 'skin' of brass plates was fastened. Most life-sized or smaller bronze statues were made using the lost-wax method, involving the preparation of a full-sized clay statue, or part of a statue for large pieces; this was covered with wax, which is then surrounded by another clay layer, resulting in a 'sandwich' of clay with a thin layer of wax between. This is then fired, so that the wax melts; the space in which it had been is filled with molten bronze. Once cool, the outer layer of clay is removed, leaving a bronze sculpture that replicates the form of the original clay. Further detailed working of the metal was done when cold. It has been suggested that this method may have been used to create individual elements of the Colossus, which were then hung from the iron frame; others believe the structure was made of hammered bronze sheets rather than cast.

The monumental statue stood on a 15-metre (49-ft) high marble plinth, 18 metres (59 ft) in diameter. Atop the pedestal, the feet of the statue were carved from stone and then covered in bronze; eight iron bars rose from the stone ankles, linked by curved bronze plates that formed the beginning of the legs. An earthen ramp gave access to the ever-rising statue. Chares probably learned this technique of creating monumental sculpture by assisting his master, Lysippos, to build another colossal bronze, this one a 22-metre (72-ft) -high statue of Zeus and a seated Herakles for the city of Tarantum (modern Taranto), in southern Italy. Pliny describes Lysippos as having made around 1,500 works during his career, all of them in bronze. Though many marble Roman copies after his lost originals exist, the only possible original that survives is the so-called Victorious Youth, also known as the Getty Bronze, displayed in the Getty Museum in California.

Chares' Colossus met a more natural fate. It stood for only fifty-four years before a violent earthquake struck the island in 226 BC, destroying much of the city. The Colossus broke at the knees, toppling over and crashing backwards to the ground. Ptolemy III of Egypt offered to pay for the restoration of the statue, but enquiries made at the Oracle of Delphi revealed that the earthquake was the result of the Rhodians having offended Helios, the sun god, so they declined the offer. The Greek historian and geographer Strabo (c.64 BC–AD 23) wrote that in his day the broken body of the statue, and the stone feet and plinth, still lay exactly where they had fallen.[8] In its broken state, the colossus was a destination site for curious travellers. Pliny the Elder wrote that a grown man would have trouble wrapping his arms around a single fallen thumb of the statue, so giant had it been.[9] It was only in AD 653 that an Arab army under Muawiyah I captured the island of Rhodes and, according to Theophanes the Confessor (d. AD 818), melted down the bronze in the statue. A Jewish merchant from Edessa is said to have bought the metal, requiring 900 camels to carry it off.[10]

In 2008 the Greek government announced plans to rebuild the Colossus as a sculpture of light. Despite the ensuing political and economic turmoil in Greece, the plans were still alive in 2015, though it is not clear when or if the statue will actually rise again above the harbour at Rhodes.[11]

The Lighthouse of Alexandria

Few remains of the wonders of the ancient world still survive, and the list of seven (which stabilized in the Renaissance but was based on numerous examples of such lists developed by Classical travel writers, recommending what to see and describing the sites to those who could not journey to them in person)[12] includes only one that can still be seen in its entirety:

The six pyramids of the Giza complex; from left, the three largest are the pyramids of Menkaure, of Khafre and of Khufu (the Great Pyramid), built between c.2575 and 2465 BC

the Great Pyramid at Giza. The Hanging Gardens of Babylon (see chapter 9) is the only one that is not known to have been destroyed, since it is not certain if it ever existed. Another two, like the Colossus of Rhodes, fell victim to natural disaster and subsequent decay.

Ptolomy I Soter (the Greek successor to Alexander the Great as ruler of Egypt) ordered the construction of a lighthouse (*pharos*) in the harbour at Alexandria, in the Nile Delta, which was built between around 286 and 246 AD. The structure comprised a limestone tower with a furnace at its peak, the fire in which was used to signal vessels approaching the harbour. It stood between 103 and 118 metres (338–387 ft) high, on a base that was 30 by 30 metres (98 × 98 ft) square. It was damaged in a series of earthquakes beginning in AD 956; a final tremor in 1323 left it in ruins. Many of the stones from which it was built were used to construct the Citadel of Qaitbay in 1480, but evidence for fragments of the lighthouse were discovered in the harbour at Alexandria 1968; in 1994 a team of underwater archaeologists, lead by Jean-Yves Empereur, began systematic excavation of the site at the bottom of Alexandria's Eastern Harbour, recovering

Imaginary reconstruction of the *Pharos* (Lighthouse) at Alexandria; painted copper engraving after a drawing by Johann Bernhard Fischer von Erlach, *c*.1700

five obelisks, thirty-two sphinxes, six columns of the Egyptian dynastic period, a Roman Corinthian column capital and some column bases. In 2015 the Egyptian Supreme Council of Antiquities announced plans to rebuild the lighthouse.

The Mausoleum of Halicarnassus

According to Pliny, the Mausoleum at Halicarnassus was an elaborate tomb that was built for Mausolus of Caria, who died in 355 BC, by his widow (and sister), Artemisia. She died in 353 BC, and the tomb was completed after her death. Mausolus was a satrap, or regional governor, of the Persian imperial outpost of Halicarnassus, on the south-west coast of what is now Turkey. He lends his name to all later mausoleums (now a term for any above-ground tomb), of which this was the predecessor. A rectangular structure, 32 × 38 metres (105 × 125 ft) and up to 40 metres (131 ft) high, it was decorated

Imaginary reconstruction of the Mausoleum at Halicarnassus, 1882, engraving

all around with freestanding statues and sculptural reliefs, the latter depicting battles between the Lapiths and the centaurs, and between the Greeks and the Amazons. The appearance of the tomb has been debated for centuries, and there are many widely varying reconstructions. Ancient descriptions state that each side was carved by a different renowned Greek sculptor – Timotheus, Bryaxis, Skopas of Paros and Leochares (Skopas was also the architect of another of the ancient wonders, the Temple of Artemis at Ephesus). The tomb was said to have been capped with a loggia with ten columns on each side and a massive pyramidal sloping roof with a flat platform at its peak. Perched at the top was a *quadriga*, a sculpted chariot drawn by four horses. The *quadriga* may be similar to that currently displayed at Basilica San Marco in Venice; it once stood in the Hippodrome in Constantinople and was first looted during the Fourth Crusade (1204).

The mausoleum survived numerous attacks on the city – by Alexander the Great in 334 BC, by pirates in 62 and 58 BC – and stood watch over the port for a good 1,600 years. Sadly, a series of earthquakes from the twelfth to the fifteenth century reduced it to ruins, and by 1404 it was reported that only the base was still intact. Some of the rubble from the mausoleum was integrated into the structure of Bodrum Castle, built in 1494 by the Knights of Saint John of Rhodes, while the rest was used to expand the city's fortifications in 1522, in anticipation of an Ottoman invasion. The main burial chamber, uncovered by the knights during this last excavation, was empty, having been looted by grave robbers via an underground tunnel at some point in the distant past. The knights recycled the remaining sculptures for plaster, burning the marble to produce lime, though a few statues were removed and displayed at Bodrum Castle. It was the longest lasting of the six destroyed wonders of the ancient world.

Aquila and Assisi

Even today's admirable technology, which can sometimes predict earthquakes before they happen, cannot protect monuments great or small. In 2009 a quake rated 5.8 on the Richter scale devastated the city of Aquila, in Italy's Abruzzo region. The

Conservation work being carrid out on the frescoes (1297–1300) by Giotto in the Chiesa di San Francesco, Assisi, after the earthquake of 1997

cathedral lost part of its transept, the third floor of the Forte Spagnolo Castle, which housed the National Museum of Abruzzo, collapsed, and the cupola of the eighteenth-century church of St Augustine were among the prominent monuments damaged. At least 308 people died, and in 2012 six scientists and one government official were convicted of manslaughter for having downplayed the likelihood and magnitude of the earthquake, theoretically preventing possible evacuation or other actions that might have led to fewer casualties. The verdict was overturned in 2014, but the case only highlights how, even in an age in which we can often predict natural disaster, human response can be insufficient to mitigate the situation.[13]

An earlier earthquake, in 1997, wrought havoc on the Umbrian town of Assisi, devastating the world-famous frescoes by Giotto (c.1270–1377) and other luminaries at the Basilica of St Francis of Assisi. A team of conservators was tasked with salvaging the frescoes and bringing them as nearly as possible back to their former, pre-quake state. When the frescoes in the Chapel of St Nicholas were displayed again following restoration, the effort was considered to have been a success. Conservator Bruno Zanardi, who was not a member of the team working at the site and was therefore considered an objective voice, said that he 'saw the site in 2011, and got the impression that it was a good job'. But when he returned in 2015, his opinion shifted. 'I had a very different impression', he told *La Repubblica* newspaper.[14] Other key figures in the art world were dismayed by what they saw. Francesco Scoppola, who led the Ministry for Cultural Heritage team overseeing the repair, was 'most alarmed', because the *chiaroscuro,* the dramatic contrast of light and shadow, appeared to have been lost, such that the restored frescoes were much more monotone and flatter than Giotto's originals, particularly one showing the Virgin Mary fainting before the cross.[15] But this may be subjective.[16] The earthquake had brought down a thousand tons of debris on to the church, so the squabbling over subtleties of light and shade seems rather pedantic; it is a small miracle that the frescoes survived at all, and in a state sufficient to prompt jibes about the quality of shadow-play.

And just in case one doubts that 'acts of god', such as earthquakes, might have a penchant for striking at the work of Giotto, consider this: in 2014 another Giotto fresco cycle, at the Arena Chapel in Padua, was struck by lightning, mangling an iron cross atop the chapel, which acted as a lightning rod. Thankfully, the art within was not harmed.[17]

SEA AND SALT:
THE FONDACO FRESCOES OF VENICE

It is a bad idea to paint in fresco in a city immersed in seawater. The humidity of Venice is such that frescoes fade and the plaster on which they are painted begins to flake off within only a few decades of their completion. Vasari wrote in 1550, 'For myself, I know of nothing more harmful to fresco painting than the sirocco, especially near to the sea where it carries a salt moisture with it.'[18] In Venice, only mosaics last. But while they did last, the frescoes that once adorned the exterior of the city's Fondaco dei Tedeschi were a destination for visitors and point of pride for Venetians.

The Fondaco (derived from the Arabic term for 'storehouse') was a centre for foreign merchants, the Fondaco dei Tedeschi for those of Germanic origin (the term encompassed much of northern Europe, not just modern Germany). On the Grand Canal near the Rialto Bridge, it was a warehouse for goods and a place to do business, and the upper floors also contained living quarters for foreign merchants in Venice on business. The building was originally constructed in 1228, but the one we see today dates to 1508, following a fire that consumed the earlier structure. The year it was completed, a dazzling series of frescoes was unveiled on the facade facing the Grand Canal, painted by a pair of young Venetian artists, the greatest of their generation, Titian (1490–1576) and Giorgione (1478–1510).

Giorgione and Titian were the rising stars of the studio of the master Venetian painter Giovanni Bellini (1430–1516), but shortly after they completed the Fondaco frescoes, their careers careened in very different directions. Giorgione was dead within two years, cut down by plague. He made very few works in his abbreviated career (the number of surviving works ranges from fewer than twenty to forty, though the exact quantity is debated), so anything by Giorgione is hugely valuable – far more than a work by his wildly prolific, long-lived friend. Titian lived to be eighty-six, was master of a large and thriving studio for decades and produced scores of paintings; his influence extended to the court of Spain. There are mysteries surrounding the relationship between Giorgione and Titian, and some have even theorized

Giorgione, *Nude*, 1507–8, fresco, from the facade of the Fondaco dei Tedeschi in Venice, now in the Galleria Franchetti, Ca' d'Oro, Venice

Top: Giorgione, *The Triumph of Justice*, possibly Judith with the head of Holofernes, 1507–8, fresco, from the facade of the Fondaco dei Tedeschi in Venice, now in the Galleria Franchetti, Ca' d'Oro, Venice; the outline of a figure in German armour is at bottom left
Bottom: Giorgione, *Battle Frieze*, 1507–8, fresco, from the facade of the Fondaco dei Tedeschi; the scene may represent the ninth labour of Hercules, in which the hero had to kill the carniverous birds of Stymphalis, in Arcadia, shown as huge beasts with crane-like necks

that Giorgione might not have existed at all, and was actually Titian's pseudonym.[19] Conspiracy theories aside, the two were stars of Bellini's studio, with Giorgione the more advanced in years and stature at the time the Fondaco was painted. After he died, probably in October 1510, Titian finished several of his paintings (exactly which, and to what extent, also remains debated). Thus the legacy of the two remains intricately linked, but nowhere more so than in a fresco cycle we can no longer see, thanks to the relentless Venetian humidity. In 1966, what remained of the paintings was removed and transferred to the safety of the Ca' d'Oro, a mansion on the Grand Canal that became a public gallery in 1927; since then, scholars have sought to reconstruct the fresco cycle.

As with most things related to Renaissance art, the first stop was Vasari's *Lives of the Artists*. He describes a seated woman holding a sword and the severed head of a giant (surely Judith with the head of Holofernes, though she might represent Germania, an embodiment of the German people), 'speaking to a German standing below her'.[20] This was the focus of the cycle, painted above the main doorway of the Fondaco. A seventeenth-century print, ostensibly based on the fresco, shows as much, with the German in armour, concealing a dagger behind his back. (One wonders what message the German merchants of Venice were hoping to convey, if indeed this was the main image above the entrance to their warehouse.) There is a more serene and elegant *Judith with the Head of Holofernes* by Giorgione in the Hermitage, painted in 1507, which could be linked to the fresco. Above the seated Judith/Germania figure were a pair of female nudes, another figure accompanied by the head of a lion, and a putto (a form of cupid) holding a short staff and painted near some apples. Some have suggested that the frescoes referred to the Twelve Labours of Hercules, which would make the seated woman Alcmena, Hercules' mother, and the severed head that of Eurystheus rather than Holofernes; the lion would represent the Nemean lion, the putto is Mercury, the apples refer to the golden apples of the Hesperides stolen by Atlas, and so on.[21] It is a compelling idea, but frustrating – we just don't know. The frescoes themselves are too fragmentary, derivative works (such as prints made after the frescoes) are incomplete or of suspect accuracy, and the textual references (such as those by Vasari) must be taken with a grain of salt, as we do not know how complete or accurate they are, or if Vasari actually saw the paintings in person.

When completed, the Fondaco was a wonder of Venice, and the frescoes the talk of the city. They covered the facade, wrapping around the windows, integrating the architectural elements and including some painted *trompe-l'oeil*. They solidified Giorgione's reputation, and helped to launch the career of Titian. But the damage that the sirocco salt wind wrought within decades of their completion means that their influence and memory was fleeting. A Venetian artist called Zaccaria dal Bo (1872–1935) made watercolour sketches in the nineteenth century of what was left of the frescoes; they are atmospheric but lack detail, probably because the frescoes themselves lacked detail by that point. The Fondaco dei Tedeschi paintings are one of the great invisible masterpieces, a key to history but one which has long ago melted away against Venice's hot canals and saline breezes.

Zaccaria dal Bó, sketch of the frescoes by Giorgione and Titian on the facade of the Fondaco dei Tedeschi, 1896, watercolour on cardboard, 31.5 × 39.8 cm (12¹/₂ × 15³/₄ in)

FLOOD:
TREASURES LOST TO THE ARNO MUD

That the surviving frescoes of the Fondaco dei Tedeschi were transferred out of harm's way in 1966 was serendipitous, for that was the year the flooding of the river Arno ruined much of the art of Renaissance Florence.

Eight serious floods had been recorded in Florence since 1333 (oddly, three of them struck on the same day, 4 November), but the flood of 4–5 November 1966 was by far the worst.[22] An estimated 2.5 metres (8 ft) of rain – some 44 per cent of the annual normal precipitation – fell over two days. The banks of the normally tranquil Arno burst, and the tightly grouped wonders of the Renaissance that cluster in the small city centre were suddenly, unexpectedly and simultaneously endangered. The basilica of Santa Croce, dating from 1296, was the worst affected, standing almost 3 metres (10 ft) deep in river water.[23] A total of 101 people lost their lives, but most of the world's attention was focused on rescuing the city's art. Volunteers who flew in from around the world became known as the *angeli del fango*, 'mud angels' – for when the rain finally stopped, most of their work involved carefully excavating books, manuscripts, artworks and masonry from within metres of thick mud mixed with oil and sewage.

By some estimates, millions of cultural objects were lost: around 3 million books and manuscripts and some 14,000 moveable art objects, of which 1,500 or so were significant artworks.[24] Masterpieces ruined include Paolo Uccello's fresco *Creation and Fall* (1443–6) and Andrea di Bonaiuto's *The Church Militant and Triumphant* (c.1369), both from the church of Santa Maria Novella, and the mighty wooden *Crucifix* (c.1288) by Cimabue, forefather of Renaissance Florentine painting. Hanging in Santa Croce, where the water level rose to 4 metres (13 ft), it was so waterlogged that it swelled more than 7 centimetres (3 in).[25] The paint flaked off, as did pieces of wood. Removed from the water, the cracks worsened, the wood grew mouldy, and paint continued to fall away. The object still exists, restored with poplar wood from the Casentine forest, the same forest from which Cimabue's original wood came, but it remains scarred and torn, a symbol of what was lost. The mudflows (some 600,000 tons of mud, sewage and rubble) also endangered seminal works such as Donatello's *Penitent Magdalene* (1455) and Ghiberti's *Gates of Paradise* (1425–52), three panels of which were ripped from their mounting. Giorgio Vasari's monumental, five-panel *Last Supper* (1546) was caked in the mud that engulfed Santa Croce, where it had hung for four centuries.[26]

From the tragedy emerged some important positives, however.[27] The Opificio delle Pietre Dure (literally, 'Workshop of Semi-precious Stones') was established in Florence and is now one of the world's foremost institutes of art restoration and conservation. And in the wake of the flood, new techniques for preserving manuscripts and detaching frescoes from walls were developed.[28] Restoration technology had advanced around this time in terms of analyzing art with various light spectra (such as X-rays), but the physical manipulation of damaged art, including cleaning and restoration and, most important, preventing further deterioration, had seen relatively little major improvement before 1966. Suddenly the world's attention was focused on salvaging art that often was not portable.

Giorgio Vasari, *Last Supper*, 1546, oil on panel, undergoing restoration in the refectory at the basilica of Santa Croce; the painting was submerged in flood waters for more than twelve hours, the lower sections for even longer

Conservators dealt with multiple problems with panel and canvas paintings: cleaning works of mud and debris, reattaching flaking paint and keeping the supports from contorting too much in the humidity changes were the primary concerns. One technique, used in the immediate aftermath of the flood on water-damaged works on panel, such as Vasari's *Last Supper*, was to apply strips of Japanese mulberry paper to the painted surface, brushed with a layer of methacrylate resin to make them stick. This method was used to reattach bits of paint that had flaked loose when the underlayer of gesso, a plaster made of animal glue, grew unstable due to moisture. (It would turn out to be difficult to remove the mulberry paper without taking the paint with it, but this was an emergency triage attempt, and the problem was eventually resolved successfully in 2010.)[29] Works were allowed to dry slowly, but changes in humidity inevitably led to curvature of the wooden supports (the painted panels or the wooden framework behind the canvas) and caused the paint to crack. Ciro Castelli, a twenty-three-year-old carpenter recruited as an emergency restorer in 1966 (now a senior conservator) came up with a technique to prevent the panels

Cimabue, *Crucifix* (c.1288), distemper on wood, 448 × 390 cm (14 ft 8 in × 12 ft 9¹/2 in); photograph from 1966 shows the tragic damage done to the medieval artwork following flooding and then drying

contracting too much, by stuffing a filler of poplar wood into incisions made on the back of the panel.[30]

Then there was the issue of getting damaged frescoes off of walls. By definition, a fresco is a painting in which pigment is applied directly to wet plaster on a wall or ceiling, and so the painting is an integral part of the building on which it is painted. A technique to transfer frescoes, with their plaster intact, on to a portable support was developed in Florence after the 1966 flood and is now the most successful and commonly used method (it was used to remove the Titian and Giorgione frescoes from the Fondaco dei Tedeschi); it is called the 'strappo technique' (*strappo* is Italian for 'I tear'). A linen cloth is applied to the fresco and painted with a diluted glue made of boiled animal bones; this attaches the paint to the linen, but in a way that is reversible, without damaging the paint itself. The final coat of plaster on to which the fresco was painted, called the *intonaco,* is then, with surgical precision and painstaking slowness, cut away from the rest of the wall with a scalpel. The result is a 'sandwich' of linen, paint and the *intonaco* layer of plaster. The back of the plaster is then pumiced to smoothness and covered with canvas, and the linen front is moistened. Once wet, the bone glue in the linen releases its grip on the paint, and the fabric can be peeled away. Thus, what was once an integral part of a plastered wall becomes a painting, still attached to a thin layer of plaster, but now affixed to a fresh canvas, for display in a museum.

The strappo technique for remounting frescoes is a far more sophisticated version of a method described by the Roman writer Vitruvius as having been in use in 59 BC in Sparta: 'paintings have been taken out of certain walls by cutting through the bricks, [then] enclosed in wooden frames'.[31] Interestingly, wall paintings that had been transferred to wooden frames were also found in the ruins of Pompeii.[32]

—

Early spring, 1738. East of Naples, a new palace for a new king is being laid out at Portici. Amid the noise of stonemasons and the stink of the mules hauling carts of ash for lime, two men take it in turns to dig a well from which the royal household will drink. The ground is hard as cement, and the men sweat and curse in the sun. On the third day an ancient statue is pulled from the hole – a small bronze of a dancer in swirling drapery. Another shovelful of dirt exposes a battered silver bracelet with amethyst beads. 'Best package these up and send them to the king', says the foreman. The men dig deeper.

The first of the towns buried by Vesuvius was initially 'rediscovered' in 1709, when two ancient statues were recovered by well-diggers, but the significance of the find was not understood. When more ancient remains were seen while another well was being dug in 1738, however, Charles III Bourbon, King of Naples, decided to explore further. As a result, dozens of metres below the eighteenth-century town of Resina, the lost city of Herculaneum began to come to light again, after nearly 1,700 years. Pompeii followed in 1748, and fifteen years later the name of the ash-drowned town was revealed, when excavators unearthed an inscription reading REI PUBLICAE POMPEIANORUM.[33]

These early excavations were carried out not by trained archaeologists (a science that did not exist in the eighteenth century), but by architects and engineers subject to Charles III. (The king was an avid collector whose private collection of antiquities would go on to form the basis of the Museo Archeologico Nazionale in Naples.) The Swiss architect Karl Weber (1712–64) and the Spaniard Francesco La Vega (1737–1804) supervised the uncovering of several sections of Herculaneum and Pompeii, keeping detailed diaries filled with drawings of what was found and where. These records of the earliest excavations are valuable pieces of information for archaeologists and historians, having been created at a time when most visitors were merely interested in finding and absconding with buried treasure. The excavation found its stride during the French occupation of Naples (1806–15), when a systematic approach to the work began to be imposed;

some 1,500 workers were employed, and Pompeii was dug out
from west to east, revealing the most important public sections,
including the forum and several bath complexes. Three-quarters
of the city had been revealed by 1860, but archaeologists are still
finding things to this day; less than half of Herculaneum has
been uncovered.

One surprise was the ornament and colour everywhere.
The image of ancient Rome at the time was of pure, white marble
and ivory-hued travertine. But ancient Rome, like ancient Greek
cities, were explosions of colour, with gaudily painted temples and
the walls of buildings from baths to brothels to palaces decorated
in fresco or jewelled with mosaic.

Pompeii and Herculaneum helped scholars to understand
the nature and extent of Roman wall painting, which archaeologist
Crispin Corrado describes as 'villa scenes, still-life motifs,
seascapes, playful images of cupids engaged in the daily
activities of their human counterparts, and portraits of family
members on the walls of bedrooms. The Romans painted full-
sized architectural vistas with perfect depth and perspective,

Nineteenth-century photograph of excavations at Pompeii

and one clear and consistent vanishing point.'[34] Artistic techniques were remarkably advanced, demonstrating concepts that had to be relearned by Renaissance artists, having been forgotten during the Middle Ages. Corrado suggests that the so-called Large Oecus (room 15) of the Villa of Poppaea at Oplontis illustrates best the wonders of Roman wall painting. 'Not only do we see convincing perspective and a consistent vanishing point on the east wall', he says,

> but we also see a detail that shows how careful, how masterful these painters were. Look closely at the flutes on the two columns that surround the central doorway in the centre of that painting, and you will see that the flutes cast shadows, as if they were truly three-dimensional. This is something the did Romans routinely in their wall paintings: paint in shadows, as if the architecture were true and freestanding. But there is more. Across examples, ancient wall painters were careful to match up the direction of the falling shadow with the light source in the room. In this case, at Oplontis, the window in this room opened to the sea and was situated to the right of the painted wall. That means the light was coming in from the right. If the columns had been real, not just painted, and freestanding, their three-dimensional flutes would have cast shadows in the direction opposite to the light source: the shadow would have been cast behind the flutes, to the left. In fact, this is where the shadows were painted. The painting is convincing even down to this tiny but magnificent detail.

Fifteenth-century artists such as Donatello and Brunelleschi spent years in Rome studying ruined statues and buildings, with the goal of rediscovering the lost techniques of the ancients. They did so successfully, with Donatello resurrecting the lost-wax method of making thin-skinned bronze sculpture, and Brunelleschi using Roman engineering techniques to successfully build what was then the world's biggest dome, above Florence's cathedral.

Lost (and found) Roman buildings, and the art that decorated them, not only influenced artists but completely altered the

Above: Reception room (*tablinum*) at the Villa of Poppea, Oplontis; the eastern wall is painted with a fresco depicting a shrine of Apollo
Opposite, top: Detail of the shrine of Apollo fresco, showing the tripod of the Delphic Oracle
Opposite, bottom: Detail of the shrine of Apollo fresco, showing the painting's careful perspective and decorative theatrical mask and fresco

concept of what the ancient world looked like. Excavations on the Athenian acropolis around 1832 contributed to what became known as the 'polychromy debate'. Residual pigments were found on the ancient buildings, suggesting that they had been brightly painted, contrary to traditional thinking. The exposure of Pompeii and Herculaneum ended the argument, showing the painted ancient cities in their original glory.

TEMPORAL WORKS

*Amsterdam's De Appel gallery, an evening in 1976. A crowd
has gathered in a dimly lit room to witness what the artist calls
'photographic objectivity'. Attendants ensure that everyone
is inside before closing the doors to the interior space without
windows. Voices falter, and a few final giggles are silenced. There
is only the sound of breathing in the darkened room. Suddenly,
yellow-green lights like those used in photographic darkrooms
are intensified to reveal nine large photographs on three of the
four walls.*

Performance art is designed to be temporal. There may be relics
of the events or the destructions-as-art (photographs, written
accounts, videos), but the real thing took place at a specific time,
for a short duration, in a particular place. You were there, or
you were not.

The observers of the performance *Fototot I*, staged by the
conceptual artist Ulay (b.1943) at De Appel, witnessed the
murder of photographs.[1] The nine photographs on the walls
of the gallery – showing images of the artist himself, disguised,
wearing a hat and an overcoat, a scarf covering most of his face,
standing at various distances from the camera on a dirt road –
had been processed, but not fixed. The result was that when the
light hit them, they quickly faded into nothingness, their content
evaporating into blackness. It took between fifteen and thirty
seconds for the photographs to fade – just enough time for the
crowd to register the content of the images before their *fototot*,
or 'photo-death'. A second performance, *Fototot*, was staged a
few weeks later for the same audience and featured a portfolio
on a table in the middle of the gallery, with a reading light above
it. The portfolio contained photographs taken of the first action,
also unfixed. When the audience switched on the reading light
to view the pictures, they encountered the disconcerting image
of themselves disappearing.

These linked performances offer commentary on the
fragile and changeable nature of photography. Ulay began his
career running a photography studio in post-war Germany,
where he grew up, before moving to Amsterdam in 1970 to
work as an artist. In 1968, he became one of the first official
photographers for Polaroid. This was a time, pre-Photoshop, in

which some governments, for example that of the Soviet Union and Communist Czechoslovakia, were selectively 'airbrushing' history – chemically removing from photographs images of individuals they wished to erase from collective memory.

The Czech novelist Milan Kundera's *The Book of Laughter and Forgetting*, written two years after *Fototot*, opens with just such a scene. He describes a photograph taken on 21 February 1948, in which two figures, Vladimir Clementis and Klement Gottwald, stand side by side. When Clementis was charged with treason in 1950, the state had him erased from the photograph. Thus the assumption that photographs were true records of history and the camera an objective recording machine was shaken.

Standing in the darkened room at De Appel, the gallery goers may have felt like they were standing inside a camera, a black box into which light is briefly admitted when the photographer clicks the shutter button, projecting an image on to the film inside; if this film is further exposed to light before it is developed and fixed, that image is lost. The production of

Ulay, *Fototot I*, 1976, De Appel gallery, Amsterdam; initial presentation, before fading

an image is the artist/photographer's exertion of domination over the camera. In *Fototot*, the artist seemed to tease both the audience and the camera itself, taking some effort to develop and display the prints, only to have them disappear, intentionally, within seconds of their being seen. Ulay has said that 'without destruction there is no creation', and this performance is a literal example: creating photographs in order to destroy them as part of an artwork. And while most performance art is built around the actions of the performer, the star of the show, in this case Ulay was not visible at all – an illusionist in his own disappearing act.

If this were not conceptually rich and complex enough, there is more. Because *Fototot I*, like all performance art, is staged only for the audience *in situ*, in the right place at the right time, the only records of it are photographs taken during the event, and oral histories passed on by the artist or those who attended. Photographs of disappearing photographs. Performance art appears briefly, only to vanish.

Ulay, *Fototot I*, 1976, De Appel gallery, Amsterdam; the photographs after having been faded to black by exposure to light

—

One of the great frustrations of studying art history is to learn
how many marvellous-sounding works are lost. There are
hundreds of works that were described by contemporaries as
wondrous, but which were only ever meant to be temporary.
Renowned artists spent a disconcerting amount of time and
energy on installations and decorations for major festivities;
weddings, banquets, tournaments, victory parades and the like
called for artists to create backdrops, sculptures, even entire
buildings that were only meant to last the duration of the
event, after which they were disassembled or discarded. Some
magnificent decorations were documented in paintings, but
in most cases we have only tantalizing descriptions penned
by awed contemporaries. The works are long gone.

EPHEMERAL WORKS FOR COURT AND CHURCH

The role of Jan van Eyck (1390–1441) as court painter required his participation in a wide variety of ephemeral painting and design-related enterprises apart from wall and panel painting. Indeed, panel paintings were low priority for court painters, whose primary tasks involved wall painting to decorate official residences, manuscript illumination, and design for aristocratic and royal events. There are strikingly few references to panel paintings in Flemish court inventories, an indication of their limited value. In the main, only portraits, kept as historical records, would be assigned to court painters. Court artists such as Jan van Eyck in the Duchy of Burgundy or the Florentine Giorgio Vasari (1511–74), who served numerous popes but was worked primarily for Cosimo de'Medici, were more often tasked with making elaborate, expensive stage sets for festivals or other events, works that were never intended to endure. A modern equivalent might be the opening ceremony of the Olympic Games. The festivities for the 2012 London games, designed by film director Danny Boyle, cost some 27 million pounds sterling, all of which, along with the intensive preparations, went into a single, spectacular performance, preserved only in pictures. In the 1454, Philip of Burgundy held a banquet, called the Feast of the Pheasant, at which a huge pie was rolled out of the kitchen. The pie contained 'twenty-eight people, who were to play on different musical instruments, each when his turn came'.[2] It is almost certain that designing banquets such as that, along with the decoration of foodstuffs, occupied most of van Eyck's time. It is a bit heartbreaking to imagine what wonders he came up with that were temporal, and so lost to us, and what wondrous paintings he might have created for posterity, had his time not been consumed with dressing men up as birds to jump out of baked goods.

Georgio Vasari was also tasked with designing decorations for major events, such as the visit of the Holy Roman Emperor Charles V (1500–58) to Florence and the 1539 wedding of Vasari's patron, Cosimo de' Medici, to Eleonora di Toledo. These were chances to impress visitors with the talents of local artists at a time when galleries, in the modern sense, did not exist. Aside from choreographed visits to palaces and churches, visitors were unable to see the treasures produced by, in this case, the cream of Florence's artists; ensuring a good impression made the temporary decorations for aristocratic events worth the investment of time and money (as frustrating as this might be for later generations). For the wedding of Cosimo and Eleonora, which took place in Bologna, Florentine art had to be transported and showcased in Bologna before the couple moved to Cosimo's city. Vasari was one of dozens of artists and artisans recruited for preparations. He spent a month working on a huge cartoon (a full-sized preparatory drawing), and would eventually paint three large-scale pictures on panel and twenty scenes from the Apocalypse (rather an unusual wedding theme).[3]

In the spring of 1567, summoned by Pope Pius V, Giorgio Vasari built a temporary structure in Rome that he described as a *macchina grandissima*,[4] an immense machine. It was a triumphal arch made of wood, installed around the main altar at the church of Santa Croce del Bosco; it held over thirty paintings in its structure, the whole of which was flanked by columns, mounted with sculptures and had a large crucifix rising out of the top.[5] Vasari described it as 'an immense machine that is almost a triumphal arch, with two large panels, one on the front and one on the back, and around thirty stories painted on small pieces of the structure, containing many figures made with the highest level of detail.'[6] The fact the he oddly refers to this as a *macchina,* a machine, suggests that it was either moveable (perhaps on wheels) or that it had moving parts (sections could be opened and closed).

Giorgio Vasari, *Macchina Grandissima*, 1567; 3D reconstruction by the Computer Vision and Multimedia Laboratory, University of Pavia, based on a painting of the structure by an anonymous artist, *c.*1575–85, and on a drawing by Vasari preserved in the Louvre

THE FIELD OF THE CLOTH OF GOLD

One of the greatest temporary works was not so much an artwork as an architectural masterpiece. The Field of the Cloth of Gold was a contest of wealth and power and codpiece size in the guise of a tournament, held between Henry VIII of England (reigned 1509–47) and Francis I of France (reigned 1515–47), for which an entire village, including a gilded castle, was built just for a few weeks.

A complicated three-way Renaissance rivalry had been brewing for years between Henry VIII, Francis I and the Habsburg ruler Charles V. It had to do with who would be elected Holy Roman Emperor, with alliances and territorial disputes, with France's anxieties about being geographically surrounded by Henry's England and Charles' extensive empire, with religious disputes and with war. But it also involved the royal egos of three almost comically masculine kings, each determined to demonstrate the might of his armies, his own physical prowess, his wealth and his erudition. The armies of Francis and Charles engaged on multiple occasions (with the French king taken prisoner at one point), and the two rulers at one point challenged each other to single combat, with their empires in the balance. Their advisors talked them out of it, but not before they had reached the point of arguing details such as weapons of choice (Francis wanted to go at it medieval style, charging with lances then finishing on foot with daggers, whereas Charles preferred rapier and cloak, a more gentlemanly approach). But the story of the Field of the Cloth of Gold concerns Francis and Henry.

On 24 June 1520, at a place called Balinghem, near Calais (then a part of England but surrounded by French territory, and therefore considered neutral ground), the two kings met, ostensibly to cement the 1514 treaty they had signed for mutual protection against Charles' extensive empire, which threatened them both. The Treaty of London, engineered by Cardinal Wolsey, was an attempt to maintain peace between the powers of Europe but was in danger of rupturing, owing mostly to the animosity between Charles V and Francis I; it was best if the two remained far apart at all times. Wolsey's plan was, first, to have Henry and Charles meet to reaffirm their non-aggression agreement, and then to have Henry meet Francis to do the same. This was to be that second meeting. The event lasted around eighteen days and featured all manner of extravagant banquets, tournaments and other entertainments. But the actual meeting was less talked about than the construction of the place in which it was to be held.

Both kings saw this as a chance to show off their wealth, culture, grandeur and fine taste. Each called in his leading artisans, artists, chefs and architects and spared no expense in overt attempts to outdazzle the other. It was a duel of sorts, but one of money and taste rather than lances and spears (though the tournament component meant that the young kings could show off their athletic prowess as well). The spectacle included both architectural and decorative elements. Henry's tournament armour was said to have been decorated with 2,000 ounces (56.7 kg/125 lbs) of gold and 1,100 enormous pearls. His confidante, the Earl of Devonshire, wore clothing woven with gold and silver, along with his entire retinue. Costume was but a minor element, however. Since Balinghem was in English territory, Henry saw the meeting as his chance to prepare an architectural masterpiece that would awe his rival.

An entire chapel was built, complete with statues of saints, reliquaries and stained glass. It was reportedly so large that thirty-five priests were required to service it. Henry's retinue was accommodated in tents bedecked with expensive silk textiles, made more expensive by being woven with gold thread. These were exquisitely fragile – a gale-force wind that prevented tournament action one day must surely have taken its toll on the fabrics, as did rain – but that was beside the point.

It didn't stop with tents. An entire palace – temporary, like everything else – was built in front of the existing castle. It was 100 metres (328 ft) long on each side, with 2-metre (6^1/$_2$-ft) high brick walls topped by 10-metre (33-ft) high wood-framed walls of canvas painted to look like brick. Even the roof was fake: it was made of oiled cloth painted to look like lead tiles. The whole was from all accounts a hugely elaborate, rather weird, ridiculously wasteful production, mostly *trompe-l'oeil*, like the set of a film. But it was not merely a facade – it was usable and, at 10,000 square meters (107,639 sq. ft), unimaginably large for

*The Field of the Cloth of Gold, c.*1545, oil on canvas, 168.9 × 347.3 cm (5 ft 6$^{1}/_{2}$ in × 11 ft 4$^{3}/_{4}$ in),
Royal Collection, Hampton Court Palace, London

something meant to be functional for only two weeks. It was also packed with art. *Grafton's Chronicle*, published in 1569, describes it in some detail:

> The foregate of the same palace or place with great and mighty masonry by sight was arched, with a Tower on every side of the same portered by great craft, and inbatteled was the gate and Tower, and in the fenesters, and windows, were images resembling men of warre redie to cast great stones: also the same gate or Tower was set with compassed images of ancient Princes, as Hercules, Alexander and other, by entrayled worke, richly limned with gold and Albyn colours, ... also the tower of the Gate as seemed was built by great masonry, ... for the sundrie countenances of every Image that there appeared, some shooting, some casting, some ready to strike, and firing of gonnes, which shewed very honorably.[7]

Two fountains inside this pop-up palace flowed with red wine, which accompanied an impressive amount of food, all brought along for the event. The number of people present was not recorded, aside from some of the aristocratic retinues (each king brought some 500 horsemen and 3,000 infantry, for starters), but we do know that 2,200 sheep were consumed, and 2,800 tents were built to house visitors who were not sufficiently important to warrant a place in the palace. Henry even brought along a pair of monkeys, a gift from the Ottoman sultan Suleiman the Magnificent, which were dressed in clothing covered in gold leaf. Francis was apparently delighted by the gold monkeys; Cardinal Wolseley described how he laughed hysterically whenever he saw them, and decreed that they should be present at every banquet.[8]

The Field of the Cloth of Gold is an extreme example of flaunting one's wealth, influence and consumable sheep for a fleeting event, all to be dismantled once the party is over. Hundreds of less elaborate artistic installations were made for other events throughout the Renaissance, distracting great artists from more permanent enterprises. On the one hand, it seems a wasteful shame. On the other hand, what a sight it must have been.

SHORT-TERM ART FOR EVERYMAN

The artist Christo (b.1935) and his wife and artistic partner, Jeanne-Claude (1935–2009), built a career out of temporary art installations that could be experienced by anyone, and which exist now only as photographs and preparatory drawings.[9] The brevity of the window of time in which they could be experienced was part of their appeal, as were their occasionally remote locations; these became the goal of a sort of artistic pilgrimage. From 22 September to 5 October 1985, the Pont-Neuf across the Seine in Paris was wrapped in 41,800 square meters (450,000 sq. ft) of sand-coloured fabric. An estimated 3 million visitors saw the work and walked over the shrouded bridge. Twenty years later, *The Gates* was erected in New York City's Central Park, comprising 7,503 framed gateways, on the crossbeams of which hung saffron-coloured fabric that flapped loose in the breeze. The work existed only from 12 January to 27 February 2005.

All of Christo and Jeanne-Claude's projects were self-financed, solely through sales of preparatory drawings; *The Umbrellas* cost 26 million US dollars. For this installation, 1,760 yellow umbrellas were installed at a ranch in Tejon, in

Christo and Jeanne-Claude, *The Pont Neuf Wrapped, Paris, 1975–85*

Christo and Jeanne-Claude, *The Gates, Central Park, New York City, 1979–2005*

southern California, while 1,340 blue umbrellas occupied land in Ibaraki, Japan. The exhibition, which would have required a trans-Pacific flight to see in its entirety, ran from 9 to 27 October 1991. Tragedy struck *The Umbrellas* on a day in which a major storm was forecast for California. A female visitor and her husband ignored police warnings to avoid the area, and strong winds blew down one of the heavy (220 kg/485 lbs) umbrellas near them. As she ran from the falling umbrella, the woman fell, hit her head, and died; several others were injured, though none was actually hit by an umbrella.[10]

ART MADE TO BE DESTROYED

Physical artworks have also been lost deliberately, created in order to be destroyed, as an integral act of completing the artwork. *Homage to New York* was created in 1960 by Jean Tinguely (assisted by Robert Rauschenberg). It was a giant machine, towering 8.2 metres (27 ft) high, and Tinguely built two of them, one for the Museum of Modern Art in New York and one, called *Study for an End of the World* (1962), for a stretch of desert outside Las Vegas, Nevada. Both were mechanical suicide machines, designed to destroy themselves automatically. A journalist from *Time* magazine, one of 250 spectators at the MoMA motorized suicide, described it: 'An hour and a half later, the suicide-fated machine started flaming and sawing at its mixed-up insides, turned balky, despite several judiciously aimed kicks from its creator, got doused betimes by an anxious fireman, and had to be finished...'[11]

This sort of destructive performance was *en vogue* in the subversive 1960s. A conference called 'Destruction in Art Symposium', held in London in September 1966, gathered together scientists, poets and artists, including Yoko Ono and

Jean Tinguely, *Study for an End of the World, No. 2*, 1962, auto-destructive work, dimensions variable, Tinguely Museum, Basel

Gustav Metzger. As part of the proceedings, the conceptual artist John Latham (1921–2006) constructed three vertical towers of books dubbed *Skoob Towers* ('skoob' being 'books' backward), outside the British Museum, ultimately setting fire to them.[12] The performance piece was part of Metzger's Auto-Destructive Art movement, which the Bavarian artist had launched in England in 1959; Latham's *Skoob Tower Ceremonies* took place in various locations between 1964 and 1968. Metzger's article entitled 'Machine, Auto-Creative and Auto-Destructive Art' – a commentary on the needless ravages of war, bringing in elements of Dada nihilism and playful mischief – appeared in the avant-garde magazine *Ark* in 1962.[13]

—

John Latham, *Skoob Tower Ceremony*, Bangor, North Wales, March 1966

The Museum of Modern Art in Ljubljana, Slovenia, 2012. An audience, including the author, shuffles into an interior room without windows. A work of lost art is about to be resurrected, and this time the visitors know what to expect. Conversation slowly dies away as they await, again, the death of photography.

What happens when a temporal work of performance art, once (intentionally) lost, is found again? The arrangement that evening was familiar to all of us who knew the 1976 version of Ulay's *Fototot*. The only major difference was that this time the room was pitch dark before the lights came on and the images in the photographs disappeared before our eyes. For a few unrepeatable moments, an intentionally temporal, lost work of art, the subject of which was the idea of 'losing' art, was found again. But only momentarily. This element makes performance art, as the name suggests, a theatrical piece, with a brief, maybe even one night only, run. Recordings remain (video, photographs, spoken or written recollections from those present), but that is all. The only way such lost artworks can be found again is if the artist is willing to re-enact, as in this case. The freshness and originality of the initial performance is lost,

Ulay, *Fototot II*, 2012, performance, Museum of Modern Art, Ljubljana, Slovenia; the artist is in the foreground

but none of the magic of being in the midst of a magician's act, one both intellectually complex and exciting to participate in. The fragility of the fading photographs and the realization that you can see them for only a few precious seconds is a powerful potion, inciting an adrenaline rush, a thirty-second episode of Stendhal Syndrome, a thundering appreciation of a long-dead, long-anticipated artwork that can be viewed for such a terribly short time.

DESTROYED BY OWNER

Leonardo Sellaio moves his candle closer, dips his quill into a pot of ink and inscribes the date on a small sheet of rough paper. 5 February 1518. The scratch of the quill whispers in the silence of the empty studio as he writes to his master, Michelangelo Buonarroti, acknowledging the instructions to have all Michelangelo's full-scale drawings and preparatory cartoons incinerated. 'It pains me, but your will is to be done.'

Giorgio Vasari mentions Michelangelo (1475–1564) burning drawings only 'at the end of his life', but this letter from his assistant Sellaio is evidence that he was doing it regularly.

Vasari was one of the first proactive collectors of drawings as an art form worthy of preservation and display. The Renaissance painter, architect and biographer of his fellow artists gathered drawings by many of the peers he admired and included them in his *Lives of the Most Eminent Painters, Sculptors and Architects* (1550), considered the first art history text. In addition to collecting biographical information for his *Lives*, he collected drawings as relics of the artists themselves, and found in them insight into each artist's creative processes. One of the greatest of all lost art treasures is Vasari's own *Libro de' Disegni*, or *Book of Drawings*.[1] It began with Vasari's receipt of a collection of drawings that had been assembled by Lorenzo Ghiberti (1378–1455), the great Florentine sculptor. Vasari enriched and expanded this collection in a multivolume series of blank books into which he pasted drawings by artists ranging from Cimabue to Michelangelo. He would sketch his own drawings in the margins around the originals, inspired by them and paying homage to their style. It was a sort of personal, portable museum, made at a time long before the modern concept of an art museum had formed. It would be several centuries before dealers and collectors began to seek out drawings for themselves. At this point they were considered merely preparatory sketches for paintings and sculptures, rather like blueprints compare to a house. You keep the house, but you don't necessarily save the blueprints.

In sixteenth-century Italy, artists took great pains not to show or admit to the effort involved in creating great works. The term *sprezzatura* translates as an easiness of manner, a studied

Giorgio Vasari, page from *Libro de' Disegni*, sheets c.1480–1504, mounting and framework by Giorgio Vasari after 1524; includes drawings by Filippino Lippi, Sandro Botticelli and Raffaellino del Garbo, with decoration in brown ink, brown and grey wash on paper, 56.7 × 45.7 cm (22¹/₄ × 18 in), Private collection

carelessness, the giving off of a sense that what you do comes to you easily, without any sweat, metaphorical or otherwise (described most famously in the dialogues in Baldassare Castiglione's popular 1528 publication, *The Book of the Courtier*). The cultural emphasis on *sprezzatura* led Michelangelo to destroy scores of his own drawings, feeding them into a fire to obliterate the reams of preparatory sketches over which he laboured to ensure that his final paintings and sculptures were as perfect as his audience found them to be. After publication of the updated, 1568 edition of his *Lives,* Vasari also published a slim excerpt, dealing only with the life of Michelangelo, entitled *Vita de' gran Michelagnolo Buonarroti,* in which he wrote:

> .... I know that, a little before he died, he burned a great number of designs, sketches and cartoons made with his own hand, to the end that no one might see the labours endured by him and his methods of trying his genius, and that he might not appear less than perfect.[2]

—

The origins of the proactive collection of art by specific artists is linked to Vasari and his era. His *Lives* helped develop the cult of the artist-genius and the desire for collectors to own a work by a particular hand, as opposed to the earlier norm of desiring a certain sort of artwork, say an Annunciation painting, and then deciding on which artist to commission. Nevertheless, the art trade and the extraordinarily high prices for art that continue to this day, which make us wonder at buyers or creators who voluntarily destroy objects that can be worth millions, really took off in eighteenth-century England.

COLLECTING FOR PLEASURE AND STATUS

In England, the practice of collecting was fuelled by the foundation of private galleries and auction houses. Sotheby's was founded in 1744, Colnaghi's in 1760, Christie's in 1766. The single most significant event for the development of art collecting came in 1792, with the dismemberment of the art collection of the Duc d'Orleans. The dismantling of this aristocratic collection, which had included over 500 paintings and scores of engraved gems, mostly acquired by Philippe d'Orleans between 1700 and 1723, allowed these relics to be purchased by those with aristocratic aspirations or illusions. The *nouveau riche* middle class sought elevation towards the *ancien regime* in which taste and nobility were thought to be innate; by adopting the trappings of those who, in financial straits despite their blue blood, were forced to sell their collections, the new owners captured the constellations that adorned the world of the aristocrats. In contrast to the 1649 Commonwealth Sale of the goods of the executed English king Charles I, which was politically symbolic of the dismantling of the *ancien regime* by force, this redistribution of goods from an impoverished aristocracy to a new moneyed class was a cooperative enterprise, though one that would ultimately favour the latter. The *nouveau riches* had money, but their social position was an artificial and precarious construct. The accumulation of art objects originally collected by 'legitimate' aristocrats solidified the foundations of social position that the new owners sought to construct. Even today, when a work of art is sold with the name of a prominent past owner listed among the provenance, its value skyrockets.

Beginning in 1857, before private collections were made public in a more formal way, the British Institute in London held an annual exhibition at which recent acquisitions by private collectors could be displayed to the public. This ostentatious display of wealth, taste and social position through the prism of purchased works of art is indicative of collecting at this time. It was no longer merely a private pleasure, but was now a chance to show one's greatness to the public – generally, an audience of peers whose opinion was valued by the collector.

By the 1840s, collectors had become a stock character in modern cities, parodied in cartoons and literature. As Oscar Vásquez wrote, 'the collector as a subject was evident in almost every sector of western European society, and collections now included objects previously unrecognized as collectable.'[3] Balzac's *Cousin Pons* (1847) and Flaubert's *Bouvard & Pecuchet* (1881) feature collectors as protagonists, and tourists published volumes on their visits to private collections abroad, for example Gustav Waggen's *Treasures of Art in Great Britain* (1845) and Johann David Passavant's *Tour of a German Artist in England* (1836), much to the delight of the collectors praised in print. The identity of the collector was represented by the objects in the collection: 'In reality the objects coveted by the collector express his eternal pursuit of himself.'[4] Collections were attempts at self-completion, inevitably linked to desired social status. Art objects could provide a solid foundation for the social heights that each collector believed he deserved to inhabit.

Private collectors opened their doors to visitors deemed worthy – for the most part, social peers and foreign literati. As Vásquez wrote,

> Even while many of the nineteenth-century private collections remained secluded, unpublished and closed to public scrutiny, their meanings and values would nevertheless have been altered by the transformations of cultural and economic values conditioning those collections that were opened ... Classifying, recording, preserving of collections through the instruments of state-mandated inventories, estate partitions, and entailments and their archives can be seen as extending already extant classifications of social structures.[5]

Mid-nineteenth-century discourses on collecting stress accessibility to private galleries for critics and art historians, but they also promote the social element of collecting.

Collecting for Profit

In *The Order of Things* (1966), Michel Foucault speaks of the phenomenon of taxonomia, which is perfectly manifested in the art collection. It involves the desire to classify and arrange, thereby creating an identity and hierarchy both for the collection itself and, by extension, the collector. The collected object's meanings are constructed not only in relation to other objects within the collection, but to all other collections.

The temptation to resort to criminal means to enhance one's own collection, or deprive another's collection of a trophy, has sometimes been too difficult to resist. The blurring of the separation between art and money has also contributed to art crime. When art objects began to be equated in the public eye with their purchase price, the criminal element took notice. The opening of the private collections to varying levels of public scrutiny, and the purchase of works of art from high-profile galleries and auction houses, led to the discussion and publication of the monetary values of works of art. While the art itself rarely excited popular interest, the money involved in its acquisition did, and by extension, made celebrities of the artworks and their collectors.

Art crime was a more visible problem in some places than others. William George Clark, a British traveller in Spain, wrote the amusingly titled *Gazpacho; or Summer Months in Spain* in 1851, in which he noted, 'Half of Seville lives on pictorial thefts and forgeries; not a day passed that I was not pestered with people offering for sale fragments of broken altar-screens; and half the saints in the calendar painted on oval bits of zinc and copper.' By contrast, in London, the centre of the art market at this time, criminality flowed beneath the surface, interwoven with legitimate transactions.

Collecting for Museums

The eighteenth and nineteenth centuries were also the era of the foundation of the first national museums. The British Museum was established in London in 1753, the Belvedere in Vienna in 1781, the Louvre in Paris in 1793, the Rijksmuseum in Amsterdam in 1808, the Prado in Madrid in 1819, the Altesmuseum in Berlin in 1823, and the National Gallery in London in 1824, funded by a grant of 7500 pounds sterling from Sir George Beaumont (1753–1827). The John Julius Angerstein picture collection was bought by Lord Liverpool on behalf of the nation, forming the backbone of the collection. Before the sale, Beaumont expressed concern in a letter to Lord Dover:

I would rather see [the Angerstein picture collection] in the hands of his Lordship than have them lost to the country, but I would rather see them in a museum than in the possession of any individual, however responsible in rank or taste; because taste is not inherited, and there are few families in which it succeeds for three generations. My idea is, therefore, that the few examples which remain perfect can never be so safe as under the guardianship of a body that never dies...'[6]

Thus the seed was planted for a 'body that never dies', a national art gallery. After Lord Liverpool bought the collection for the nation, Beaumont wrote again to Lord Dover: 'I think the public already begin to feel works of art are not mere toys for connoisseurs, but solid objects of concern to the nation.'[7]

It is interesting to hear the opinion that taste is not inherited. This takes the hereditary power of taste away from the aristocracy and gives hope to wealthy members of the middle class that they might become men of taste, even one day aristocrats themselves. The Morgan family, discussed in chapter 1, pursued Gainsborough's *Portrait of Georgiana, Duchess of Devonshire* for just that reason. By acquiring art that had been, at least nominally, linked to a forgotten branch of the family tree, they obtained not only a trophy of their present wealth and erudition, but a tangible 'proof', of sorts, of an aristocratic heritage – the only thing that money could not buy.

With all this in mind, not least considering the financial investment involved, it seems bizarre that some owners would voluntarily destroy a work in their possession.

Those who wilfully destroy valuable art do so for a variety of reasons. Rarest are the collectors who, after paying for a work, choose to obliterate it. More common are artists who destroy a work in order to create a new one. More common still are artists who destroy creations they decide they dislike, are embarrassed by or which reveal too much, as in the case of Michelangelo's incineration of what, in today's market, equates to hundreds of millions of pounds' worth of drawings.

DESTROYED BY PATRON

Throughout the history of portraiture, the wise artists flattered to deceive. There is an unattributed saying that a great portrait should reveal a hidden truth about the sitter, but one so well hidden that the sitter will not see it, and will still pay for the painting. Whatever the artist may think of the sitter, that sitter is ultimately the one who has to be pleased in order for the artist to be paid. Portraitists did not always like those they portrayed (Goya was famously unimpressed with Charles IV of Spain), and those portrayed were certainly not always physically beautiful. Clever artists worked around aesthetic imperfections to provide reasonable likenesses in which the objectionable bits were 'airbrushed'. Federico da Montefeltro had a ruined right side of his face, courtesy of a nasty jousting wound, so Piero della Francesca (d.1492) portrayed him in strict profile in a portrait of 1472–3. Fortuitously, this also mimicked the profile portraits of ancient emperors on coins, but the point was more about masking than historical reference. But it was rarely the style of the painting that rubbed patrons the wrong way, for the portraitist was selected, after all, on the basis of past work. It could become an issue, however, when a third party chose the artist.

Graham Sutherland's Portrait of Winston Churchill

Winston Churchill was no Adonis, but most of his portraitists did what they could to flatter him. However, when British artist Graham Sutherland (1903–80) was commissioned to paint a full-length portrait of Churchill in 1954 for the handsome fee of 1,000 guineas (about 26,900 pounds sterling today), paid by the

Graham Sutherland, *Winston Churchill*, 1954, oil on canvas, destroyed 1955

House of Commons and the House of Lords, and the work was presented in a lavish public ceremony, things did not go well.

Sutherland was a well-respected modernist painter, chosen not by Churchill but by members of the Houses of Parliament wishing to honour his long tenure and service on his eightieth birthday. Churchill initially liked the idea and asked to be portrayed in the robes of a Knight of the Garter, an order of which he was proud to be a member. The commissioners, however, specified that he should be portrayed as he most commonly dressed when visiting Parliament. Sutherland prepared for the portrait by making charcoal sketches of his subject's face and hands on several occasions at the Churchill home at Chartwell, in August 1954. (Hands and faces have always been considered the most difficult to get right. In the studio system, in which commissions were designed and overseen by a master but often painted by other members of the workshop, hands and faces were usually reserved for the master himself.) For inspiration, Sutherland referred to one of Churchill's many memorable quotes: 'I am a rock.'

The result, when it was revealed on 20 November 1954 to Clementine Churchill, was not a smashing success. While Lady Churchill was said to have remarked that it looked 'really quite alarmingly like him', and Churchill's son, Randolph, thought it made his father look 'disenchanted', the sitter himself hated it at once. On seeing a photograph of it, he called it 'malignant ... filthy'.[8] Ten days before the official presentation, he wrote to Sutherland, rejecting the painting altogether and declaring that the ceremony would not include it. He was only persuaded with great difficulty, after much cajoling by MP Charles Doughty, to accept the portrait at the ceremony in order to avoid causing offence. The presentation was to be televised on the BBC, which meant that Churchill was obliged to compliment the painting, though he did so with faint (or one might say feint) praise, saying that it displayed 'force and candour' and was 'a remarkable example of modern art'. One of his political opponents described it as 'a beautiful work', while an ally dismissed it as 'disgusting'.

The work was destined for permanent display in the Houses of Parliament after Churchill's death, but it was initially given to the Prime Minister as a gift. It was destroyed shortly thereafter,

with news of its obliteration emerging only in 1978. Lady
Churchill had hidden the portrait away in the cellar at Chartwell;
at her request, the Churchills' private secretary, Grace Hamblin,
arranged for it to be removed by night and burned secretly on
a bonfire.[9] Word came forth that this was not the first Churchill
portrait that his wife saw fit to condemn: portraits by Paul Maze
and Walter Sickert similarly disappeared under her watch.[10]
Sutherland considered the destruction of his painting an act
of vandalism, but when one considers that portraits, particularly
official ones destined for public display, have always been a
combination of visual record and propaganda, it is perhaps
unsurprising that a likeness the subject did not consider
flattering, in a style he disliked, should have been suppressed.

Diego Rivera, *Man, Controller of the Universe*, 1934, fresco, 4.85 × 11.45 m (16 ft × 37 ft 6 in),
Palacio de Bellas Artes, Mexico City; copy of Rockefeller Center fresco after its destruction

Diego Rivera's *Man, Controller of the Universe* and the *Detroit Industry* murals

Man at the Crossroads (renamed *Man, Controller of the Universe* when it was repainted in Mexico) was a mural created in 1934 by the Mexican painter Diego Rivera (1886–1957) and was the star attraction at the Rockefeller Center in New York – until the Rockefeller family had it destroyed.

Politically conservative John D. Rockefeller Jr. perhaps chose poorly when he decided to work with Rivera, a member of the Mexican Communist Party, but he was commissioning one of the most famous and talented artists of the era. The original preparatory sketch showed three men holding hands at the centre of a vast, multifigure design – a soldier, a peasant

and a worker. The sketch was approved, but when Rivera began to paint the final work on the wall, he changed the content without getting approval. What happened next has been the subject of much debate, but a 2014 exhibition, 'Man at the Crossroads: Diego Rivera's Mural at Rockefeller Center', held at the Mexican Cultural Institute in Washington, DC, suggested that Rivera was scorned and teased by his left-wing colleagues and the Communist groups with which he sympathized for having 'sold out' to an exemplar of conservative capitalism. The artist decided to undermine his own patron, allegedly instructing an assistant to find a picture of Lenin from which he could work, saying, 'If you want communism, I will paint communism.'[11]

When the work was revealed, the headlines did nothing to soothe the Rockefellers. The *World Telegram* wrote: 'Rivera Paints Scenes of Communist Activity and John D. Jr. Foots the Bill'. Adding insult to injury, Rivera included a portrait of Rockefeller, drinking martinis with a 'harlot' – a scene that his son, David Rockefeller Sr., later said his father found thoroughly unflattering. The orientation was such that Lenin was on one side and Rockefeller on the other, and Lenin came out looking the better of the two. Since the work was a fresco, painted directly on to wet plaster and therefore an integral part of the wall, it could not simply be scraped off. In an attempt to resolve the issue, Rivera was asked to remove Lenin, but the choleric artist claimed that he would 'rather see the work destroyed than mutilated'. In the end, the mural was chiselled off the wall.

The Rockefellers should have known what they were getting into. Rivera's previous murals in the United States, depicting the Ford Motor Company in Detroit and finished just a year earlier, were very nearly destroyed after a scandal. German art critic Wilhelm Valentiner hired Rivera to create a huge fresco cycle, twenty-seven panels in total, for display at the Detroit Institute of Arts. The cycle was meant to show all aspects of Detroit's booming industrial landscape, at the time the largest in the world. The idea of honouring workers made Rivera, with his Marxist tendencies, a good choice. He was also arguably the biggest name in American painting at the time, having just completed a widely praised mural at the California School of Fine Arts, *The Making of a Fresco Showing the Building of a City*

(1931). The Detroit Institute of Arts would pay for the work, with Edsel Ford, of the Ford Motor Company, contributing 20,000 dollars.[12]

Rivera was meticulous, spending three months researching industry in Detroit, visiting factories and making hundreds of preparatory sketches. He completed the commission in eight months, a remarkably short time for a work of this scale; it required working seven days a week, with many assistants, often for fifteen hours a day. It was said that the burly Rivera lost 100 pounds (45 kg) during this time.[13]

The cycle was begun in 1932, in the midst of the Great Depression, and the local political climate was not one that supported the funnelling of tens of thousands of dollars into a painting, particularly one made by a foreigner when a quarter of the workers in Detroit had lost their jobs and work was being shifted abroad to places like China. A 'hunger march' was staged by striking workers at the Ford plant, stones were thrown, scores were injured and there were several deaths at the hands of police.[14] Rivera's politics ensured that he supported the strikers, at the same time that he was being paid by their boss, who occupied the role of villain in the dispute.

At the ceremonial unveiling of the murals, many of those present found things to be offended by, including Rivera's depiction of the Holy Family, with Joseph shown as a doctor and Mary as a nurse, Joseph giving the Christ Child a vaccination; the Three Magi appear as scientists. There were calls for the works to be destroyed, as many felt they represented pro-Marxist propaganda erected callously in the heart of capitalist America. *The Detroit News* called the murals 'vulgar ... un-American'.[15] The Detroit Institute of Arts felt compelled, decades later, to erect a disclaimer beside the murals, which began with the words 'Rivera's politics and his publicity seeking are detestable'.[16] This may be the first time in history that a commissioning institution felt the need to condemn an artist while admitting that the art was beautiful, important and worth preserving.

Diego Rivera, *Detroit Industry*, 1932–3, fresco, lower panel 5.4 × 13.7 m (17 ft 8¹/₂ in × 45 ft), Detroit Institute of Arts, Illinois; the Holy Family scene appears at upper right

Vincent van Gogh's *Portrait of Dr Gachet*

On 15 May 1990, Japanese businessman Ryoei Saito bought van Gogh's *Portrait of Dr Gachet* (1890) for 82.5 million dollars. Two days later, he bought the smaller of two Renoir paintings entitled *Bal du Moulin de la Galette* for 78.1 million dollars (the larger canvas hangs in the Musée d'Orsay in Paris). He later announced that he wished to have the van Gogh painting cremated with him when he died. Colleagues tried to explain that this was just a figure of speech, expressing the owner's passion for the work, but the art world was concerned that one of van Gogh's

Vincent van Gogh, *Portrait of Dr Gachet*, 1890, oil on canvas, 67 × 56 cm (26^1/$_2$ × 22 in), whereabouts uncertain

masterpieces would be lost. Saito later stated that he would consider giving it to a museum in his will, but the painting has not been seen since; Saito died in 1996. Reports surfaced in 2007 that the businessman had sold the painting to an Austrian collector, Wolfgang Flöttl, who had later sold it on,[17] and its whereabouts remain unknown. A second version of the portrait, which van Gogh (1853–90) was thought to have painted as a gift for Dr Gachet, is displayed at the Musée d'Orsay, though the authenticity of this version has been questioned: examination showed that this version contained underdrawings, contrary to van Gogh's normal process of applying paint directly to blank canvas.[18]

The Renoir painting was used as collateral for loans to Saito's businesses, and was sold by the banks concerned when those businesses experienced financial difficulties. It is believed to be in a private Swiss collection, but has not been seen since 1990.[19]

DESTROYED BY ARTIST

The practice of artists destroying their own work is almost exclusively a phenomenon of the modern era. Prior to the eighteenth-century rise of galleries and the art market, and especially before the industrialization of paint production, when pigments could finally be purchased for reasonable sums of money in tubes or canisters, raw materials for paintings and sculptures were so expensive that it would have been foolish to destroy them. Works were also almost exclusively made on commission; they did not sit in an artist's studio until a buyer or exhibitor could be found. So aside from irregular incidents, such as Botticelli offering his own paintings to Savonarola's Bonfire of the Vanities in a fever of piety (see chapter 4), artists before the modern period could not afford to ruin what they had made.

Before the modern period, artists very often preserved materials by reusing them. During the Renaissance, vellum and paper for drawing were not inexpensive; they were not nearly as costly as painstakingly planed and joined wooden panels, but they were nevertheless a commodity not to be disposed of profligately. As a result, paper and vellum are frequently filled with sketches, front and back, in any blank space. Canvases might also be reused, and modern technology permits us to look beneath the top layers of paint, to view what lies beneath.

Kazimir Malevich

In 2015, X-rays taken of Kazimir Malevich's iconic *Black Square* (1915; Malevich back-dated many works, so this date is debated) revealed not one, but two hidden paintings beneath it.[20] The lowest, original image on the canvas is described as a colourful Cubo-Futurist work, with which Malevich (1878–1935) experimented around 1910; the style melded the Cubist technique of fracturing an image into geometric forms seen from multiple points of view with Futurist concepts of

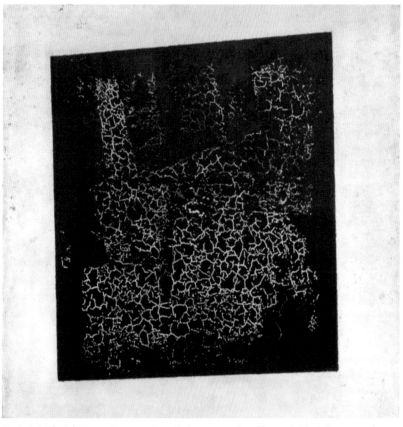

Kazimir Malevich, Proto-Supremacist painting, *c.*1910, found beneath *Black Square*, as shown on screen at a press conference held in November 2015 by the Tretyakov Gallery, Moscow

breaking free from the past and striving for entirely new aesthetic vocabularies. On top of that painting, but beneath *Black Square*, a proto-Suprematist composition was revealed. Suprematism is the movement spearheaded by Malevich, which rejected representational art in favour of monolithic geometric forms – of which *Black Square* is the textbook example. Largely erased from the white space around *Black Square*, conservators also found a bit of Russian text in Malevich's hand, which seems to read, 'Negroes battling in a cave'. This has been interpreted as the concept behind *Black Square*, perhaps inspired by an 1897 painting, also a black square, by the French writer Alphonse Allais, entitled *Negroes Fighting in a Cellar at Midnight*.

Kazimir Malevich, *Black Square*, 1915, oil on canvas, 80 × 80 cm (31¹/₂ × 31¹/₂ in), Tretyakov Gallery, Moscow

Black Square was conceived as the ultimate negation of the traditional religious icon; in doing so, it became a new form of icon. A black square inside a white square, the black is now beautifully textured (some might say ruined – it was poorly stored for decades) due to *craquelure* (the cracks made by the expansion and contraction of the pigment due to time and humidity), but originally it was smooth and matte. Absolute black is all colours, like absolute white is none, but in both cases, there is no form; indeed, Malevich called it 'zero of form'. The work was first shown in the 1915 exhibition '0, 10: The Last Futurist Exhibition of Painting'. Futurism, the largely Italian movement spearheaded by Tommaso Marinetti (1876–1944), promoted a complete break from past, from history and traditions, and the development of a new type of art, even to the point of destroying all museums and libraries in order to wipe the slate clean. For Malevich, the rejection of traditional, formal art was a statement of independence in keeping with revolutionary mood of the time.

Pablo Picasso and Claude Monet

Studying paintings with X-rays, ultraviolet and infrared lights can reveal pictures, buried but still lively, beneath surface layers of paint. If light causes the surface layers to fade, these pictures can ghost to the surface, gradually appearing as hazy outlines called *pentimenti,* as can be seen in the painting of a child suckling at the breast of his naked mother, beside an ox and lamb (perhaps a sort of Nativity scene), found beneath Pablo Picasso's famous Blue Period *Old Guitarist* (1903– 4).[21] In such cases, technology is the key to summoning up these revenants.

Like Malevich, Picasso (1881–1973) sacrificed some of his paintings in the name of art. A 1956 French film entitled *Le mystère Picasso,* directed by Henri-Georges Clouzot, with cinematography by Claude Renoir (grandson of the painter Pierre-Auguste Renoir), featured precious footage of the artist at work. Among the works he was filmed making were an ink painting of a dove with an olive branch in its mouth and a female face in its torso, and another of a bearded painter portraying a nude female who lies beside him. *Le mystère Picasso* was one of only two films to show the artist at work (the Belgian production

Pablo Picasso, *Old Guitarist*, 1903–4, oil on canvas, 123 × 83 cm (48$^{1}/_{2}$ × 32$^{3}/_{4}$ in), Art Institute of Chicago; X-ray image reveals a Nativity underpainting

Bezoek aan Picasso ('Visit to Picasso') also did so in 1949), and it was no mere documentary, but a film of the highest quality, winning the Cannes Film Festival Special Jury Prize; in 1984, the French government declared the film a national treasure.[22] The paintings that Picasso made on camera were destroyed after filming – they would only ever exist on film.[23]

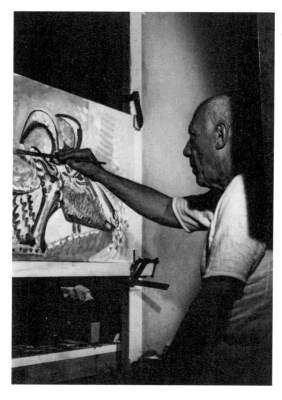

Still from the film *Le mystère Picasso*, 1956

While patrons have only occasionally condemned art to oblivion, it happens more frequently with artists, who are not always satisfied with their work. A fire that broke out at the Museum of Modern Art in New York in 1958 was largely contained, but six paintings were damaged, including two of Monet's *Water Lilies*. But even more were lost to the artist's own hand. In 1908, shortly before their scheduled exhibition at the Durand-Ruel Gallery in Paris, Monet (1840–1926) decided he was sufficiently dissatisfied with what he had produced, and he destroyed fifteen of the canvases.[24]

Gerhard Richter and John Baldessari

Like Monet, Gerhard Richter (b.1932) is a perfectionist.[25] In an early phase of his work, in the first years of the 1960s, he made paintings based on photographs, intentionally blurred as if out of focus. According to the artist's own account, displeased with the results of these finished paintings, he first cut them up with a box cutter and then burned around sixty of them in a trash heap. By today's estimates, with Richter as one of the most expensive of all contemporary artists, they would have a sales value of some 655 million dollars. Richter expressed mixed emotions about destroying the works, and he took time to photograph them before committing them to dismemberment and immolation. He told *Der Spiegel*, 'Sometimes, when I see one of the photos, I think to myself: That's too bad; you could have let this one or that one survive.' But, he admits, 'cutting up the paintings was always an act of liberation'.

We will never know how many works were discarded or recycled by artists over the centuries without a second thought, in search of art that represents the way the artist wishes to be seen now, garnishing the historical record of their work. Until a work is displayed or sold, until it leaves the artist's hand and enters the world beyond, it is reasonable (if a shame, from an art lover's or historian's perspective) that an artist may select what will emerge from the studio and what will never appear.

John Baldessari (b.1931), known primarily as a conceptual artist, felt the need to reinvent himself when he had trouble selling work. To start anew, he decided to incinerate his paintings made from 1953 to 1966 in an event entitled *The Cremation Project* (1970), which took place at a morgue.[26]

Robert Rauschenberg and Willem de Kooning

While travelling through Europe and North Africa in 1952–3, Robert Rauschenberg (1925–2008) gathered interesting bits of trash to arrange in early collages of the sort that he would later call 'combines', which would make him famous. He sold what he could, primarily through galleries in Florence and Rome, but rather than have to seek storage for them, or ship them back to his home in the Unites States, he dumped many of the unsold ones into the river Arno in Florence.[27] Only thirty-eight from this period are known to survive.[28] In 1953 he also did a sort

Robert Rauschenberg and Willem de Kooning, *Erased de Kooning*, 1953, traces of drawing media on paper with label and gilded frame, 64.14 × 55.25 cm (25¹/₄ × 21³/₄ in), San Francisco Museum of Modern Art

of performance artwork in which he acquired a drawing by the Abstract Expressionist Willem de Kooning (1904–97) and erased it, calling the resulting blank piece of paper *Erased de Kooning Drawing*. The San Francisco Museum of Modern Art catalogue entry for this work, which they acquired in 1998, reads 'drawing ... traces of drawing media on paper with label and gilded frame'. There were no known photographs of the de Kooning drawing prior to its erasure, but the museum conservators used digital technology to enhance the traces of what had been erased.

Rauschenberg's action, which one writer described as 'genteel iconoclasm',[29] is loaded with symbolism. A collector is entitled to destroy art that he has legally purchased, but if an artist destroys the work of another artist, the result is a new work of art. In this particular case, de Kooning approved beforehand. Rauschenberg is said to have gone to de Kooning's studio and expressed his interest in erasing one of his drawings as an artistic act; de Kooning, intrigued, offered him one. In fact, the older artist played along eagerly, deciding that it was not sufficient to give Rauschenberg a drawing he would have discarded anyway, nor one in pencil, which was too easy to erase completely. Instead, he provided a multimedia work that included both ink and crayon. Rauschenberg devoted a month of off-and-on rubbing to get the paper mostly clear.

Heather Benning

There are also artists who create a work, then determine to destroy it in the name of creating a new work. In 2007, the Canadian artist Heather Benning (b.1980) built a life-sized dollhouse, called *Field Doll,* from an abandoned farmhouse. Over the course of eighteen months, she renovated the house, creating an idyllic structure with picture-book rooms and one entire side of the building missing, dollhouse-style, and replaced by glass, so the rooms could be easily seen. It was a beautiful object, surreal in its magnification of a child's toy, an interesting take on our curiosity about other people's lives, at a time when reality TV was popular. But the foundations of the house, which dated to around 1968, were unstable by 2013. Recognizing the inevitability of an eventual collapse, Benning decided to turn this potential disaster into a new work of art. While beautiful

Top: Heather Benning, *The Dollhouse: Dusk #3*, 2007, printed 2011, Kodak Endura digital C-print, 50.8 × 76.2 cm (20 × 30 in)
Bottom: Heather Benning, *The Dollhouse: Fire #2*, 2013, Kodak Endura digital C-print, 50.8 × 76.2 cm (20 × 30 in)

photographs of the house remain, the building itself does not. She set fire to it that year, in a new series entitled *Death of the Dollhouse*.[30]

Jean-Auguste-Dominique Ingres

While most cases of artist-destroyed art can be attributed to a certain level of vanity or perfectionism, there were other motivations. When Ingres (1780–1867) remarried, his new spouse did not take kindly to a spectacular nude of his deceased first wife, which remained in his studio.[31] The painting disappeared, perhaps disposed of, perhaps passed on to another by the artist, in the interest of marital concord. An 1852 daguerreotype photograph of the painting in his studio is all that remains of a masterpiece.

—

Sellaio wraps his cloak closer against the cold, turns the paper over and continues his letter. 'You know of my concern that so many hold a key to the studio door. Many drawings have already been taken – by Bartolomeo Ammannati, Nanni di Baccio Bigio, Baccio Bandinelli and others who claim they steal out of love and admiration for you. They are jealous, and they wish to learn from these works the key to your success.'

Theft was not the only concern: the architect Piero Roselli wrote to Michelangelo on 4 February 1526 that he had spotted a forgery of an architectural drawing by the artist. Thus, while it was Michelangelo's desire that his own drawings be destroyed, many of them, by some estimates around 600, survived.[32] The survival of these drawings was the fortuitous result of theft, purchase, mislaying and accident that the artist himself could not prevent.

Many were preserved by Michelangelo's friend Vasari. The younger artists found in Michelangelo's drawings a summation of all that was admirable in his art, whether painting, sculpture or architecture:

[Michelangelo's drawings] showed what manner of thing is the perfection of the art of design, in executing lines,

Michelangelo Buonarroti, *Christ and the Woman of Samaria*, 1536–42, ink on gesso on panel, 77.7 × 69.9 cm (30^1/$_2$ × 27^1/$_2$ in), Walker Art Gallery, Liverpool

contours, shadows and highlights, so as to give relief to works of painting, and what it is to work with correct judgement in sculpture, and how in architecture it is possible to render habitations comfortable and secure, healthy, cheerful, well-proportioned and rich with varied ornaments.[33]

It was radical of Vasari to look so closely at drawings, to 'read' them as his peers would 'read' – i.e. interpret and study – a finished painting or sculpture. Today, drawings by great artists are just as collectible as paintings and sculptures; we have Vasari to thank for that. We also have Vasari to thank for the saving of at least some of Michelangelo's drawings, which the artist's own ego prompted him to feed to the flames so as to hide the work that went into his art, and preserve his *sprezzatura*.[34]

Hope remains that the Saito *Portrait of Dr Gachet* by van Gogh will resurface, and that more Michelangelo drawings will be discovered to have escaped the wishes of their creator. Their value as art is indicated by the prices they fetch today: in 1998, what was described as 'one of the last Michelangelo drawings still in private hands', *Christ and the Woman of Samaria* was sold at Sotheby's for 7.4 million dollars;[35] another, *Study for the Risen Christ*, sold for 13 million dollars at Christie's in 2000. These drawings provide invaluable information on the working

Aristotile da Sangallo, after Michelangelo, *Battle of Cascina*, 1542, oil on panel, 76.5 × 129 cm (30 × 50³/₄ in), Holkham Hall, Norfolk

processes of the artists who created them, used to sketch out thoughts, audition ideas and develop forms – as Giorgio Vasari knew.

In many cases, preparatory drawings exist for paintings or sculptures that were never made or are themselves lost. It is through drawings that we know how Michelangelo conceived of his never-executed *Battle of Cascina* fresco, intended for a wall in Florence's Palazzo Vecchio, to be set opposite another famous lost work, Leonardo's *Battle of Anghiari* – a dual commission intended as a sort of artist's duel, so that viewers could admire the fruits of two of Florence's greatest painters, side-by-side. Michelangelo refused to complete his fresco, because he felt at a disadvantage, having been assigned a side of the room with poorer lighting than Leonardo's; Leonardo began, but never completed, his battle scene, drawn away by new commissions. All we have is a copy of Michelangelo's drawing for the fresco, made by his pupil Aristotile da Sangallo.

BURIED & EXHUMED

24 July 2014. The desert landscape around the city of Mosul in northern Iraq is parched. In the eastern part of the city, at the ancient site of Nineveh, an explosion splits the air. The fourteenth-century minaret that stands alongside the mosque over the shrine at Nebi Yunus does not so much collapse as detonate, indicating to those who watch the scene on YouTube hours later that the structure was set with demolition charges to ensure as complete a destruction of the shrine as possible. A cloud of dust reaches into the sky.

The mound of Nebi Yunus (the Prophet Jonah) is an ancient tell, part of the remains of the Neo-Assyrian capital of Nineveh. An inscription discovered during excavations in 1852 describes how King Sennacherib (reigned 705–681 BC) built a new palace atop an artificial hill, with beams made from cedars of Lebanon, copper doors and stone sculpture. The palace was expanded and renovated by later kings, and was finally destroyed in the sack of Nineveh in 612 BC, which saw the end of the Neo-Assyrian empire. In the early Christian period, a church was built on top of the tell and, at some point in its history, the tradition developed that the mound and the church marked the site of the grave of the prophet Jonah, who according to the Bible was sent

View of the fourteenth-century Nebi Yunus Shrine at ancient Nineveh, Mosul, Iraq, before destruction by ISIS

to prophesy to the people of Nineveh. The church became a place of pilgrimage for Assyrian Christians.

In the typical manner of sacred sites remaining holy, despite changes in religion, the shrine was rebuilt as a mosque during the reign of the Mongol conqueror Tamerlane, at the end of the fourteenth century. The nineteenth-century explorer and archaeologist Austen Henry Layard would have loved to destroy the mosque in the hope of uncovering the Assyrian palace beneath, especially since he did not believe the shrine actually held Jonah's body, but cultural sensibilities deterred even this stalwart British imperialist, and the mosque was left alone.

However, to destroy a site of historical and cultural importance posed no ethical issue to the iconoclastic vandals of ISIS, who in the summer of 2014 took great care to blow up the Nebi Yunus shrine as effectively as possible. In so doing they not only destroyed the ancient mosque and its contents, but profited from it, tunnelling into the tell in search of Assyrian remains to sell on the black market.

—

Art that still exists but remains buried beneath other works is a category unto itself – lost but not. In most cases works were painted over, as painting is the medium most receptive to reusing a support: a simple recycling of materials, as opposed to the proactive desire to obliterate one work and replace it with another. While the psychological motivation behind the reuse of materials may not be of particular interest, the art very often is. The two works, plus the text, that were discovered beneath Malevich's *Black Square* (discussed in Chapter 7) show his development as an artist, the styles in which he was interested, and even suggest the dubious inspiration for his choice of an all-black painting. But this work is about more than recycling, for Malevich lived at a time when supports for paintings were not prohibitively expensive, as they were during the Renaissance, when every inch of paper was put to good use. Malevich could have simply set his older canvases aside and started a fresh one. But part of his philosophy of art, linked to the atmosphere of the Russian Revolution, was the dismissal of past art forms and the search for the new. There is, therefore, a psychological, auto-iconoclastic rationale to his painting over his earlier works, blotting them out with his Suprematist anti-icon.

MASACCIO'S HOLY TRINITY

The renovation of architectural spaces has sometimes been responsible for the loss of wall paintings until fortune has revealed them again. The famous case of Giorgio Vasari's expansion of the Sala dei Cinquecento in Florence's Palazzo Vecchio, mentioned in the introduction to this book, required his painting new frescoes over the partially completed *Battle of Anghiari* by Leonardo. There is evidence that Vasari, rather than obliterate the Leonardo, created a false wall over it in order to preserve it while fulfilling his commission. He had done this at least once before, on the other side of Florence, at the church of Santa Maria Novella.

In October 1568, Vasari's patron, Cosimo I de' Medici, instructed Vasari to alter the church. The church was magnificent, containing hugely valuable frescoes such as Masaccio's masterpiece, *Holy Trinity*, which Vasari praised for its 'simplicity and vividness' in his *Lives*. Remodelling would require obliterating or somehow moving this fresco, for Cosimo wanted Vasari to shift the rood screen (*tramezzo*) separating the nave from the chancel and bring forward the main altar, and to paint the *Madonna of the Rosary* where Masaccio's famous fresco stood. Vasari had little choice but to obey and try to figure out how to rework the space while preserving, as best he could, the wall paintings that he so admired. Someone was going to be asked to do it, and it might as well be Vasari, who was best qualified, intellectually and technically, to act as a conservationist architect:

[Cosimo] has just lately caused me to remove the *tramezzo* from the church of Santa Maria Novella, which spoilt all its beauty, and we built a new and very rich choir behind the altar, taking away the old one because it filled up the greater portion of the rest of the building. It looks like a magnificent new church, which, indeed, it really is.[1]

Masaccio, *Holy Trinity*, *c.*1427, fresco, 667 × 317 cm (21 ft 10½ in × 10 ft 4¾ in), Santa Maria Novella, Florence

Vasari's initial opinion of the project is betrayed by the start of this quote ('caused me to remove the rood screen'), but it evolved into a new project of which he was proud. The artist had a false wall constructed over the Masaccio, on which he then painted his own work. There is no record of whether preserving the older painting in this way was his own, maverick idea or whether he received permission, and the very fact that he did so was only realized in 1860, when the church was renovated. In that year the top part of Massaccio's fresco was discovered, detached from the wall, and moved to a location near the rear door. A century later, the bottom section was found, and the *Holy Trinity* was reunited.[2] One of Masaccio's most important paintings, of tremendous influence to fifteenth-century painting in Italy and long thought to have been lost, was exhumed from the grave.

Holy Trinity is one of the key works examined in any introduction to art history, owing to its striking *invenzione*, the concept behind the work. It is notoriously difficult to paint the Father, Son and Holy Spirit as one unit and simultaneously as three separate beings; God, Christ and the Holy Spirit are, conceptually, of a continuum, but must be shown in paintings as three distinct figures. Masaccio solved this conundrum by superimposing each figure upon the other. Christ hangs on the cross, God the Father looms directly behind him, and the Holy Spirit, traditionally shown as a dove, hovers between them, appearing almost like a collar around God the Father's neck. The work, finished in 1428, was hugely influential on artists in Florence (as was Masaccio's other major fresco cycle, at the Brancacci Chapel). Masaccio showcased the optical-mathematical innovation of single vanishing-point perspective early on, before it became a staple of Florentine Renaissance painting. Orthogonal lines, highlighted by the painted architectural space, draw the eye towards the vanishing point around Christ's knees in the fresco. This was radical for the late 1420s, as was Masaccio's decision to have the Virgin Mary look out of the fresco, making eye contact with the viewer as she indicates her suffering Son on the cross, reminding all who stand before the fresco that Christ died for their sins. When the work was walled up, a painting that had been visited by all who came through Florence, and that influenced a century of Renaissance artists, was lost. But thanks to Vasari's admiration for the fresco, and some clever thinking as an architect, he was able to preserve it for future generations.

RAPHAEL'S STUFETTA DEL CARDINAL BIBBIENA

Plastering over existing artworks has led to the burial of a great many works. During the Reformation, Protestants, particularly Calvinists, objected to figural representation in religious imagery and sought to destroy the 'idolatrous' trappings of Catholicism. (It should be remembered that the second of the Ten Commandments prohibits graven images, a detail Catholics preferred to overlook but which was of key importance to Protestants, Jews and Muslims). They did so literally, as is evident in the rows of headless statues of saints in churches such as Ely Cathedral and the cathedral of Lyon. Frescoes were efficiently hidden under whitewash, which modern conservation techniques have been able to remove without damaging the paintings beneath.

One case of censorship through overpainting was rather more personal. In a small toilette off the Vatican papal apartments, made for Cardinal Bibbiena (1470–1520), Raphael was commissioned to decorate the walls with erotic scenes. This was at a time when popes and cardinals often had mistresses (or young men) as secret partners, a practice periodically overlooked by the Church – so long as clergy did not marry, it was not overly concerned with their bedmates. That is, until a more pious and prudish pope came to power. Pope Leo X reigned (1513–21) when Raphael was employed to adorn the cardinal's bathing space with images of naughty nymphs chased by priapic satyrs inspired by ancient Roman painting, the mythological subject matter merely an excuse to fill a room with naked ladies. Leo was a *bon viveur*, said to have told his brother, on his election, 'Since God has given us the Papacy, let us enjoy it.'[3] He was not the sort to be bothered by such paintings, and since the greatest artist of the era, Raphael, was the hand behind them, the erotica qualified firmly as art. The bathroom was referred to as the *stufetta del Cardinal Bibbiena* – 'Cardinal Bibbiena's stove', or 'warm room'

– which might have referred to the hot baths taken there, or to the heated images on its walls.

Popes change, however, along with what they deem acceptable, and over the centuries some images were chipped off the walls while others were merely whitewashed or plastered over; the room is not today open to the public. The images that remain include Venus stepping out of a giant shell, looking at

Stufetta del Cardinal Bibbiena, Vatican; frescoes based on designs by Raphael dated to 1516

Detail of the Stufetta del Cardinal Bibbiena, Vatican, 1516; fresco showing a satyr and a bathing nymph

her naked body in a mirror, lying between the legs of Adonis (the beautiful mortal she seduced) and swimming. Cupid, her son, also appears, while a silver faucet was integrated into a painting of a satyr staring hungrily. Several other vignettes were plastered over, deemed too risqué for Vatican consumption, including one that a sixteenth-century visitor described as showing Vulcan sexually assaulting Minerva. The *stufetta del Cardinal Bibbiena* paintings were only 'discovered' by a scholar shortly before 1870; the room had been converted into a kitchen at one point but, in that year, the part of the Vatican palace in which it is located was turned into the official papal apartments, and remains so to this day.[4]

NERO'S GOLDEN HOUSE

The style and subject matter Raphael employed in the *stufetta del Cardinal Bibbiena* reference ancient Roman wall paintings that had been recently discovered, some of which decorated rooms in the emperor Nero's (reigned AD 54–68) buried pleasure palace, the Domus Aurea (Golden House). The palace was built across the slopes of the Palatine, Esquiline, Caelian and Oppian hills in Rome, after the great fire of AD 64 cleared the way. It may have covered as much as 300 acres (120 hectares) and was adorned with frescoes designed by the finest artists of the day; the main painters were Famulus and Amulius, according to Pliny's *Natural History* (AD 77–79).

Both Nero's reign and the palace he built were condemned by those who followed, and for a decade following his death items of value were removed from it and repurposed, from marble panels to statues to jewels and furniture. Next to a man-made lake, part of 2.6 square kilometres (1 sq. mile) of what had been private palace grounds, the emperor Vespasian (reigned AD 69–79), ordered the building of what the Flavian amphitheatre, known today as the Colosseum. It takes its name from a colossal statue of Nero, made of bronze and sculpted by the Greek master Zenodorus; the statue rose to a height of some 30 metres (*c*.98 ft; 106.5 Roman feet, according to Pliny), roughly the same height as the ancient Colossus of Rhodes. It was probably an athletic nude, leaning on a stone column with one bent elbow, his other hand holding the rudder of a ship perched on a giant globe, symbolizing the emperor's power over sea and land. When Nero died, the statue's face was altered so that it no longer resembled him; the sculpture was consecrated to the sun god, Sol, when Vespasian added a sun-ray crown to the head and renamed it Colossus Solis. It was moved from its position at the main entrance to the Domus Aurea to a spot beside the Flavian amphitheatre by the emperor Hadrian (reigned AD 117–38). Last recorded in the fourth century AD (having been further modified by the emperor Commodus (reigned AD 180–92) to represent himself as Hercules) it was probably a victim of the barbarian sacks of Rome. The frescoes that decorated the palace were left behind when, at the beginning of his reign, the emperor Titus (reigned AD 79–81) ordered the construction of a huge bath complex on part of the site. The rooms were filled with earth, buried along with the memory of one of the most feared and despised of all Roman emperors.

It was not uncommon for Roman locals who enjoyed a bit of adventure to break through ceilings of buried buildings and descend into them, exploring as far as they could by torch or lamplight. The frescoes they encountered on the walls were new and exciting and inspired the contemporary art of the day. The term *grotesque* refers to the type of decoration found in *grotte,* Italian for 'grottoes' or caves, designs that were adapted during the Renaissance and later Baroque periods to decorate all manner of art, from walls to furniture.

The chronological development of the wall paintings discovered in the late eighteenth century in Pompeii and Herculaneum was deciphered by the German archaeologist August Mau in the late nineteenth century. The First style, common until around 80 BC, involved painting the walls in a *trompe-l'oeil* technique to as if they faced with marble, alabaster and other valuable stones. The Second style slowly superseded the First style and was fashionable until around 20 BC; painters created elaborate landscape vistas with almost realistic perspective, seen through painted architecture that opened up the wall as if looking through a window. The Third style rejected the illusionism of the Second style but retained the architectural elements; in this style, however, those are merely decorative elements emphasizing the flatness of the wall plane, often framing detailed paintings that imitate panel paintings. The highly elaborate Fourth style was a baroque reaction to the mannerist Third style and was popular from around AD 60; it combined the large-scale pictures of the Second style with the fanciful architectural elements of the Third style, often with impossible perspectives and imaginary creatures. This was the style in which the walls and ceilings of the Domus Aurea were painted by Famulus and his team. Often incorporating faux-stucco decoration to the painted architectural divisions between narrative paintings of Third style colour blocks, the decorative designs that inspired later *grotesques* often included floral, animal or mythological elements of great intricacy and playfulness.

Luca Signorelli's (1445–1523) marvellously complex allegorical paintings, *The Calumny of Apelles* and *The Feast of Pan*, once decorated the main salon at the Palazzo del Magnifico in Siena, the palace of Pandolfo Petrucci, a wealthy merchant who ruled the city as a despot from 1487 to 1512. The ceiling was painted by Pinturicchio (1454–1513), based on designs found on the vaulted ceilings of excavated rooms in Nero's Domus Aurea. The paintings, probably finished in 1509, provided a backdrop to the wedding of Petrucci's son. When the unpopular Petrucci died, his palace was looted of its contents and allowed to fall into disrepair. Three of the frescoes from the salon – Signorelli's *Triumph of Chastity, Coriolanus Persuaded to Spare Rome*, and *Scenes from the Odyssey* (attributed to Pinturicchio) – were transferred on to canvas in order to preserve them, probably around 1843, and are displayed at the National Gallery in London.[5] Another fresco, by Pinturicchio, was removed from the room in 1843. But the whereabouts of the other two Signorellis are unknown. Were they destroyed, removed (and possibly still exist), or were they plastered or painted over and still remain in the palace, buried alive?

The term *grottesche* was first used in the context of art in a contract, signed in 1502, for the painting of the Piccolomini Library at the cathedral of Siena, work that was executed by Pinturicchio based on designs by Raphael. Raphael was

Ceiling fresco with grotesques in the form of imaginary sea creatures and bulls, from the emperor Nero's Domus Aurea, 'Golden House', c. AD 68, rediscovered in the sixteenth century

commissioned to decorate with *grottesche* the loggias adjacent to the rooms in the Vatican Palace in which he painted elaborate allegorical frescoes, including his celebrated *School of Athens* (1509–11). There is a satisfying connection linking the uncovering of long-buried ancient art, particularly in the Domus Aurea ruins, with the sixteenth-century art of Raphael: what Raphael saw while exploring the reopened rooms of Nero's pleasure palace was adapted into the pleasure toilette of a contemporary prince of Rome, Cardinal Bibbiena.

This connecting theme of inspiration applies also to another acknowledged master of the sixteenth century, Michelangelo. The covering over of the vast area of the Domus Aurea sought to erase the embarrassing memory of Nero and his indulgences, but it also served to protect the frescoes within, as well as some other treasures. One of the greatest sculptures surviving from antiquity, *Laocoön and His Sons*, was discovered in 1506 during an excavation in a vineyard near Santa Maria Maggiore, which stands on the edge of Nero's palatial estate; it was watched by Michelangelo. For him, the torqued statue of the Trojan priest who foresaw the Greek victory over Troy with the Trojan Horse was the most beautiful sculpture he had ever seen.[6] It depicts

View of ceiling fresco with grotesques in the Piccolomini Library, Cathedral of Siena, painted by Pinturicchio, *c*.1502

a moment of highest tension, when Poseidon, god of the sea and a supporter of the Greek cause, sent a sea serpent to slay Laocoön and his two sons, to prevent them from warning the Trojans about the Greek ploy. In this frozen moment of drama, the serpent is about to sink his teeth into Laocoön, whose rippling muscles in vain hold off the coils that are wrapped also around his teenaged sons; the intentional contortion of the body greatly influenced Michelangelo's own art. Mannerists, followers of Michelangelo, represented the avant-garde of mid-sixteenth-century art and owe their style indirectly to the loss and rediscovery of this ancient work. The date of the work and whether it is original or a copy of an earlier bronze sculpture has been much debated. Pliny the Elder attributes the work to three sculptors from Rhodes – Agesander, Athenodoros and Polydorus – who would have grown up in the shadow of their island's colossus. The marble statue found in 1506 is today assumed by most scholars to date to between 30 BC and AD 70; it was immediately installed at the Vatican, where it remains to this day.

Laocoön and His Sons, Roman copy of original third- or second-century BC Greek sculpture by Hegesandros, Athenedoros and Polydoros, first century AD, marble, H: 184 cm (72 in), Musei Vaticani, Rome

ORATORY OF SAINT SYLVESTER, SANTI QUATTRO CORONATI

One of Rome's most famous and best-preserved medieval fresco cycles, that of Saint Sylvester, painted around 1250, decorates a chapel adjacent to the basilica and monastery of Santi Quattro Coronati. The oratory of Saint Sylvester has for centuries been a hidden treasure on the Roman tourist trail: it is not on the normal tourist route, and one has to ring at an iron grating and

ask an embowered nun, in Italian, for a key, in exchange for a small donation, then make one's own way into the oratory. Now, however, the famous fresco cycle within, important as it is, turns out to be less intriguing than what has been hidden above it for some six centuries: an upstairs room that until 2002 was swathed in pale blue plaster.

The surviving painting downstairs shows the conversion of Emperor Constantine to Christianity through the intervention of Sylvester, and Constantine's eventual 'donation' of imperial

Fresco from the Oratory of Saint Sylvester, Santi Quattro Coronati, c. thirteenth century, showing the so-called Donation of Constantine

land as a gift to the Church. This cycle and its story carried a highly political message. It dates to a time when the papacy and the Holy Roman Emperor, Frederick II Hohenstaufen (1194–1250), were competing for primacy in Europe. Frederick felt that the Church should be subordinate to him, and that his position as Holy Roman Emperor was not that of the Church's bodyguard, but rather was embodied in the ancient term *pontifex maximus,* chief priest. The Church had other ideas, and after Frederick reneged on his pledges to participate in both the Fifth (1213–21) and Sixth crusades (from 1228), Pope Gregory IX excommunicated him. Frederick's battles with the papacy continued for the rest of his life, during which the Church was determined to establish its authority over lands claimed by the king, as well as to confirm the primacy of pope over emperor. To do so, it asserted the authenticity of the so-called 'Donation of Constantine', immortalized in the fresco cycle that survives in the oratory. The Donation is an imperial decree by which Constantine supposedly transferred authority over the Western Roman Empire to the pope. It was probably composed in the eighth century AD, and it was revealed as a forgery in 1440; but in the thirteenth century it was used as irrefutable proof of the power of the papacy over the secular emperor.

While conducting restoration work in the chapel, Professor Andreina Draghi, a specialist in the Sylvester frescoes, had wondered if there might be a second fresco cycle elsewhere in the complex, one linked to the Saint Sylvester cycle.[7] The hall above, with its blue plaster, seemed worth checking. The slow removal of the plaster took several years but immediately yielded results. Beneath lay another, beautifully preserved fresco cycle made around the same time as the cycle in the oratory, probably by the same workshop – but the subject matter was surprisingly distinct. Almost all medieval frescoes depict exclusively biblical subject matter, or images from the lives of the saints, but this cycle included both secular and pagan imagery: signs of the zodiac, allegories of the seven liberal arts and of vice and virtue (including an unusual image of armoured knights bearing saints on their shoulders), the seasons, the sun and the moon, and even Mithras, the messianic figure of a Persian religion that was popular among Roman soldiers and which rivalled Christianity

Details of mid-thirteenth century frescoes perserved behind plaster in the Aula Gotica
(Gothic Hall) above the Oratory of Saint Sylvester, Rome; these sections of the south wall
show the months with their agricultural activities

when both were minority religions in the Roman Empire. Draghi explains this odd iconography as part of the overall message of Christianity defeating evil, and more specifically of the Church defeating the ambitions of Frederick II.

Its excellent state of preservation suggests that the upper fresco was covered over within a century of its painting. Not only are the colours bright and clean, but in Draghi's opinion the walls were never retouched, whereas the Saint Sylvester cycle, visible since it was painted, was altered, restored, repainted and exposed to light and pollution all the while. The newly discovered work also looks more sophisticated and better painted than those in the oratory beneath. Draghi thinks that this could simply be down to the fact that the oratory frescoes were meddled with (though with good intention), and that these new ones thus show the quality that the Saint Sylvester cycle would originally have boasted.

The reason for hiding this cycle behind plaster is unknown, but one theory suggests that it was plastered over after a period of plague, perhaps in the belief that the unusual iconography had angered God. An earthquake in 1349 damaged the monastery and might have caused enough injury to the frescoes that it was easier to cover them than restore them (though their intact state speaks against this). Rare is the historical case study for which every 'i' is dotted and every 't' crossed. The analogy with which this book began, comparing history to an enormous jigsaw puzzle with most of the pieces missing, is just as apt for the stories of individual objects and individuals. Without a specific archival reference to the plastering of the room, scholars can only speculate, grateful nevertheless for their good fortune.

THE COLLECTION OF ERIC ŠLOMOVIĆ

There are countless stories of 'exhumed' artworks, preserved because they were been hidden. In 1949 a beautiful *Danse Macabre* fresco cycle, painted *c.*1490 by Johannes de Castuo in the tiny fortified church of the Holy Trinity in Hrastovlje, Slovenia, breathed again when the plaster that had covered it for centuries was peeled away during a renovation.

Plaster also saved art from theft during the Second World War. The Yugoslav Jew Erich Šlomović possessed an art collection of around 600 paintings, including works by Picasso, Chagall and Matisse; he acquired these while in Paris in his early twenties, where he was the protégé of the art dealer Ambroise Vollard. When Šlomović fled Paris in 1940, in anticipation of the Nazi invasion, he placed 190 paintings in a bank vault, transferring the rest to Belgrade across Nazi-occupied territories with the assistance of the Yugoslav Embassy. Šlomović was arrested shortly after and died, aged twenty-seven, in one of the mass reprisals carried out by German forces in Serbia in 1941–2.[8]

His art collection survived far longer. In 1981, the 190 works in the vault in Paris were set to be auctioned off, in lieu of unpaid banking expenses. The auction was cancelled when a legal battle over ownership of the artworks arose between Šlomović's descendants and Vollard's heirs, who claimed that Šlomović had stolen the works from the renowned dealer. A French court initially awarded the collection to Šlomović's heirs, but the ruling was later overturned in an appeal with anti-Semitic overtones; Vollard's heirs were eventually awarded everything except the artworks specifically dedicated to Šlomović by the artists. The auction of the vault's contents finally went ahead at Sotheby's in 2010, and the 190 works earned around 30 million dollars.

The 400 or so paintings that had made their way back to Belgrade were removed to a Serbian village by Šlomović and his family, in anticipation of the rounding up of Belgrade's Jews, and were hidden behind a false plaster wall in an outbuilding, where they remained undiscovered throughout the war. After the war, Šlomović's mother, cousin and other relations recovered the collection from its hiding place and were returning to Belgrade with it when a train crash killed all but the cousin, Mara Herzler. The art was described in one account as being scattered across 'a muddy field in central Serbia',[9] though Herzler insisted that the works remained in their original boxes until she was forced to surrender the collection to the Communist government of Yugoslavia in 1948. The collection has been stored at the National Museum in Belgrade ever since.

Agnolo Bronzino, *Allegory with Venus and Cupid*, mid-1540s, oil on panel, 146 × 116 cm (57¹/₂ × 45³/₄ in), National Gallery, London

THE EXHUMATION OF BURIED DETAILS

Like the wholesale rediscovery of artworks from beneath thick layers of dirt or thin layers of plaster, details of extant works are also sometimes hidden and only later revealed. When Bronzino's *Allegory with Venus and Cupid* (also known as the *Allegory of Love and Lust*; c.1545) was first displayed at London's National Gallery in the 1860s, it was deemed too sexy for the Victorian public, despite being considered a masterpiece worth admiring. To accommodate the prudishness of the time, conservators at the museum were asked to paint over some of the most titillating elements of this highly erotic painting of Venus embracing her adolescent son, Eros, while allegorical figures look on and offer warnings of the dangers of submitting to carnal lust. Eros' prominent buttocks were hidden behind a plant, Venus' erect nipple disappeared, and her tongue, which probed for her son's, was retracted. It was only in the 1980s that these Victorian additions were removed to return the painting to its original state. Such invasive alterations meant that decades of admirers and scholars misinterpreted and incorrectly described a painting that hung in front of them.

Just a few paces from the Bronzino hangs another example of a painted-over detail that dramatically alters the interpretation of a work. Hans Holbein's (c.1497–1543) famous *The Ambassadors* (1533) appears to be a formal portrait of two friends, one the French secular ambassador to the court of Henry VIII, the other the ecclesiastical representative; but the painting hides more meaning. On the two-tiered table between the two figures are instruments to read the skies and constellations (telescope, astrolabe, celestial globe) and instruments to measure or describe the earth (a ruler, books, a terrestrial globe). But if we look closely enough, all is not well. On the celestial plane, the upper register of the table, it is as we would expect; but on the earthly level, the lower register, something is amiss, a-harmonic: a single string on the lute is broken, a reference to Henry VIII's breaking with the Catholic Church and causing terrestrial disharmony. This message is further strengthened by the silver crucifix that peaks out from behind the green curtain at the upper left of the painting. This

Hans Holbein, *The Ambassadors*, 1533, oil on panel, 207 × 209.5 cm (81^1/$_2$ × 82^1/$_2$ in), National Gallery, London

Hendrik van Anthonissen, *View of Scheveningen Sands*, c.1641, oil on panel, 56.8 × 102.8 cm (22^1/$_2$ × 40^1/$_2$ in), Fitzwilliam Museum, Cambridge; before cleaning

detail was only revealed after the painting was first cleaned by National Gallery conservators in 1891 – it had been painted out at some earlier point, perhaps because it made too clear the underlying political message of this double portrait. The work is best known for the anamorphic skull on the floor of the painted room in which the ambassadors stand. It was painted in such a way that, viewed straight on, it is an indistinct blur, but when viewed from a sharp angle to the right side, the lines merge into a clear and proportionally correct human skull.

Deliberately hidden details in other works have a less obvious rationale. Hendrik van Anthonissen's *View of Scheveningen Sands* (1641), at the Fitzwilliam Museum in Cambridge, was assumed to be a well-painted but not terribly exciting landscape with a view of the sea. But when the work was sent for cleaning at the Hamilton Kerr Institute in 2014, conservator Shan Kuang described an amazing discovery: 'As I worked across the surface, a man appeared – and then next to him, a shape that looked like a sail.'[10] The 'sail' turned out to be a beached whale that, at some point prior to the acquisition of the painting by the museum in 1873, had been painted out, thus turning a historical painting into a landscape. Kuang suspects the overpainting may have been done in the eighteenth century, perhaps because the owner thought the image of the dead whale off-putting or because a dealer felt the work would sell for more without a vast animal

Hendrik van Anthonissen, *View of Scheveningen Sands*, *c.*1641; after cleaning, showing the corpse of the washed-up whale

corpse in the centre. Today, of course, the creature makes
the painting more remarkable than it had been in its simple
landscape form. Beached whales were commonly reported in the
Netherlands in the early seventeenth century, and Anthonissen's
(1605–56) painting is assumed now to record an actual event.

Paint-overs have also transmuted original works into
presumed fakes. The Carnegie Museum of Art believed that a
portrait in their collection, attributed to Bronzino (1503–72) and
thought to be of Eleonora di Toledo, wife of Bronzino's patron,
Cosimo I de' Medici, was actually a nineteenth-century forgery:
the *craquelure* on the surface did not look like a sixteenth-century
work on canvas should. The curators were so unimpressed that
they were about to deaccession the painting, but before they
doing so, their conservators took a closer look. They discovered
that although the canvas had been clumsily reworked in the
nineteenth century, it was, in fact, an original by Bronzino's star
pupil, Alessandro Allori (1535–1607) depicting Isabella Romola
de' Medici, daughter of Cosimo and Eleonora, and dating to

Sixteenth-century portrait of
Eleanora di Toledo, believed
to be by Agnolo Bronzino,
before conservation work
carried out in 2014

*c.*1570.[11] The conservator had found that while the *craquelure* was odd for canvas paintings, it was correct for Renaissance paintings on panel. A stamp on the back of the painting linked it to a nineteenth-century restorer who specialized in transferring paintings from panel to canvas. The original panel had probably cracked, and to save the painting, it was transferred to a canvas. But X-rays showed something more: while the woman visible on the repainted surface was beautiful, a much less attractive woman was depicted beneath. It is possible that the nineteenth-century reworking was to make the painting more saleable, replacing a plain subject for a lovely one.

A similar story involves a lost work by Jean-François Millet (1814–75), *The Captivity of the Jews in Babylon* (1848). It was meant to have been among Millet's most important works, carefully developed for the Paris Salon of 1848. It was received badly by the critics, however, and this lack of success inspired Millet to move away from an academic style and historical/religious subject matter, towards the style for which he would

The same portrait after conservation work revealed the orignal painting beneath later reworking: a portrait of Isabella Romola de' Medici by Alessandro Allori, *c.*1570

Top: Jean-François Millet, *The Young Shepherdess*, 1870, oil on canvas, 162 × 113 cm (63³/₄ × 44¹/₂ in), Museum of Fine Art, Boston

Bottom: X-ray image showing *The Captivity of the Jews in Babylon*, 1848, underpainting beneath *The Young Shepherdess*

Francisco de Goya, *Portrait of Don Ramón Satué* (left), and underpainted portrait of Joseph Bonaparte, 1823, oil on canvas, 107 × 83.5 cm (42 × 33 in), Rijksmuseum, Amsterdam

become famous, socially realistic genre subjects. But what had happened to the painting, no one knew. In 1984, another Millet, part of the collection of the Museum of Fine Arts in Boston, was X-rayed as part of a routine examination. To the surprise of the conservators, the X-ray showed that beneath Millet's *The Young Shepherdess* (1870), lurked *The Captivity of the Jews in Babylon*. It had been hanging on the museum's walls for decades. Scholars believe that Millet was so dismayed at the bad reception of the painting that he banished it to his family home in Normandy, where it sat for some twenty years. During the Franco-German War of 1870, it would have been difficult to get artists' materials, so Millet used what he had to hand. He painted directly over *The Captivity* – an old-fashioned, unsuccessful painting that he no longer needed to keep.[12]

X-rays also revealed a secret portrait by Francisco de Goya (1746–1828) of Joseph Bonaparte (1768–1844), who was briefly king of Spain, Naples and Sicily, and Napoleon's older brother. The portrait was found beneath Goya's 1823 *Portrait of Don Ramón Satué*, held at the Rijksmuseum in Amsterdam.[13] The macro X-ray fluorescence spectrometry that was used on the painting not only shows a greyscale image of what lies beneath the painted surface, but is a new technology (developed in the 2000s) that allows a computer to reconstruct pigments, resulting in a colour X-ray. This is key, since Goya's *Portrait of Don Ramón Satué* is a masterpiece, and no one would wish to destroy it in order to see what was beneath. The hiding of the earlier portrait was probably not necessitated by a lack of materials, as in Millet's case, but by politics. Goya was very clever about weaving around the awkward shifts in power in Spain, as a result of which he was able to work before, during and after the Napoleonic occupation of his homeland (1809–13). Still, it would have been dangerous to be known as having been an official portraitist to the Buonapartes once they were deposed, and so painting over the portrait of Joseph was probably a safety measure, literally to cover up Goya's collaboration with the French regime. In this case, 'losing' an artwork might very well have saved the artist's life.

—

March 2017. The deep blue spring skies over Mosul are clouded
with smoke as Iraqi soldiers advance, street by street, into the
western part of the city, edging closer and closer to the Great
Mosque of al-Nuri, where the ISIS 'caliphate' was proclaimed
more than two years before. In the eastern half of the city,
freed in January, archaeologists clamber through the ruins
of Nineveh and the Nebi Yunus shrine for the first time since
its destruction. Sadness and rage mix, but there is another
reaction as well: curiosity about what might now be revealed
below the shrine.

ISIS's proactive use of looted antiquities to fund their activities
has been well documented, as has their self-promotional
damaging of ancient monuments. It was assumed that in
addition to destroying the mosque and minaret at Nebi Yunus,
they would loot any antiquities they might find. But Nineveh has
been combed by archaeologists since the first excavations took
place there in 1842.[14] Any remaining artefacts would only be
found in places no one had searched before. And the only places
that had not already been the focus of archaeological search
were those for which access would require the destruction of
another important part of the site. Places like the Nebi Yunus
shrine. The archaeologists knew that the shrine was built
atop an ancient tell that had originally supported a seventh-
century BC Neo-Assyrian palace, but only the odd inscribed
brick and a few other remains had ever been found. The buried
palace had not been seen for more than two millennia.

But ISIS got there first, tunnelling beneath the ruins of the
shrine when they realized it covered another ancient building,
to reach the unseen palace and loot it of whatever portable
treasures could be found.[15] As archaeologist Layla Salih said,
'I can only imagine how much Daesh [ISIS] discovered down
there before we got here.'[16] A marble panel with an inscription
in cuneiform has been recovered; the text appears to relate to
King Esarhaddon, who ruled Assyria from 681 to 669 BC and
was the son of the palace's builder, Sennacherib. Other artworks
still in place include a large sculpture of an Assyrian demi-
goddess shown protecting mortals by scattering sacred 'water
of life' over them.

As archaeologists continue to explore the previously unknown ruins of the hidden Assyrian palace, it is hoped that more treasures, overlooked or not reached by ISIS, may be revealed. The tragic destruction of the ancient mosque and the shrine of the saint is not an event anyone would have desired, but as Eleanor Robinson, chair of the British Institute for the Study of Iraq, said, 'Isil's destruction has actually led us to a fantastic find.'[17]

Archaeologist Musab Mohammed Jassim shows artefacts and archaeological pieces in a tunnel network running under the shrine of Nabi Yunus, in eastern Mosul, Iraq, 9 March 2017

LOST, OR NEVER WAS?

From the depths of salt Aegean floods I, Poseidon, have come,
where choirs of Nereids dance in a graceful maze; for since
the day that Phoebus and I with exact measurement set towers
of stone about this land of Troy and ringed it round, never from
my heart has passed away a kindly feeling for my Phrygian
town, which now is smouldering and overthrown, a prey to
Argive might.

With this description of the destruction of the city of
Troy, the Greek tragedian Euripides opened his play *Trojan
Women*, written in 415 BC at the height of the Peloponnesian
War between Athens and Sparta.[1] The story of the Trojan
War, immortalized in the epic poems of Homer, was assumed
by the Greeks to have been history, not myth; but as centuries
passed, and the tales of Achilles and Hector and Odysseus were
told and retold, they entered the realm of fable. During the
Middle Ages, the *Iliad* and *Odyssey* were reworked in popular
medieval romances, and by the late seventeenth and eighteenth
centuries, the Age of Enlightenment, the lack of any empirical
evidence for the existence of Troy meant that most educated
men relegated it to literature, a lovely fiction dreamed up by
a blind bard. The application of logic and empirical questioning
gained momentum with the rise of historical criticism in the
early nineteenth century, in which ancient texts were plumbed
in order to learn about the worlds that had inspired the stories,
but also to test them. Textual criticism of a variety of surviving
manuscripts highlighted contradictions and inconsistencies
between them and raised questions about the veracity of
individual versions. In addition, scholars were aware that
ancient writers such as Strabo and Pliny the Elder in the first
century BC and AD recorded stories they had heard, or about
which they had read, not all of which they had personally
experienced. Thus, some of what they related or described
we now know to have been inaccurate or wholly invented. For
example, the Hanging Gardens of Babylon may well have existed,
but in Nineveh, not Babylon, as Josephus and others wrote.
Historical research and analysis meant that literary works such
as the Homeric epics were examined with deliberate scepticism
by critical historians.

And so it was for the city of Troy and the Trojan War. What the ancient Greeks and Romans assumed to have been a real place, its story transmitted via lines of poetry by a man named Homer, Enlightenment thinkers assumed to be legendary, much like the Greek myths, for lack of any corroborating evidence. The city of Troy and the acts of the Greek and Trojan heroes were worthy tales for teaching to schoolboys, and Homer's poetry some of the most dramatic ever composed, but that the events might actually bear a grain of truth, and the citadel of Troy actually exist, was dismissed.

—

I recall, as a child, browsing through a beautifully illustrated tome called *The Encyclopedia of Things That Never Were*.[2] It was full of tales of creatures, places and things that were either firmly mythological or – and this I found most intriguing – in the realm of mythical history: question marks, hybridizations, exaggerations, mis-remembrances.

Much recorded history prior to the eighteenth century was based on personal recollection or recording. Oral tradition supplied imprecise information, and archival documents provided more, along with letters and fragments of text that were essentially personal recollections. Try to remember the dimensions of the *Mona Lisa* having seen it only once, or the number of floors in the Empire State Building, and it will be clear how memories can fade, distort or evaporate altogether. Then imagine hearing a description of the Empire State Building, a place you have never seen yourself. Imagine that only your grandfather's neighbour had seen it in person, or so she claimed, and told him about it, and then he passed the story on to you.

This sort of contorted storytelling can make fact expand or contract or disappear altogether. Take the sea monster called the *kraken*, said to live off the coasts of Norway and Greenland. Its description recalls a giant squid, but it was part of the mythology of the sea long before mariners understood that the giant squid actually exists. Very occasional sightings of the huge creature were compared to the miniature versions that were common on the plates of coastal diners for millennia, and a legend developed of ships being broken apart by snaking tentacles. The legendary Yeti, or Abominable Snowman, is probably in reality the Tibetan blue bear, spotted by nervous mountaineers when it reared on to its hind legs. Travellers unfamiliar with the fauna of the Himalaya might have seen, through whipping winds and snow, what appeared to be a biped rearing up in the distance, perhaps growling, and from the logical explanation of a bear was born the Yeti legend. The tale expands with the telling: a 6-foot (2-metre) giant squid becomes a 60-foot (18-metre) squid, a growl in the snow-veiled mountains morphs into a story of having been chased by a Yeti. And so encounters with real natural phenomena are expanded into monsters.

In the course of researching this book, I came across stories of epic searches for certifiably lost art and treasure that the searchers hoped to find – as well as lost objects and places that they simply hoped existed at all. Elements of the stories behind some of these famous lost objects that might never actually have existed, usually linked to origin myths and religion, have in some cases revealed the truth behind the legend – witness the Hanging Gardens of Babylon and the labyrinth at Knossos. In other cases, a trail of concrete clues, eyewitness reports and compelling archival material suggest that tangible objects of the past, still unseen, might have actually been as the stories describe them and might possibly have survived the centuries.

LOST CITIES

Cities can be lost to natural disaster (Pompeii), fire (Rome), iconoclasm (Nimrud and Palmyra) or war (Carthage, Dresden), possibly rebuilt or definitively gone. In some cases they never entirely disappeared, in others – in areas as distant as Mexico and Egypt – they were lost even to local memory. Within a heavily forested area in the northern Yucatan Peninsula of Mexico, Slovenian archaeologist Ivan Šprajc has discovered since the 1990s over eighty lost Mayan cities.[3] Using low-altitude aerial photography, combing the images for geometric shapes peeking through the foliage that may suggest a man-made structure, he then sets out with his team, by jeep and on foot, to see what he can find. In a similar, but higher-tech approach, Egyptologist Sarah Parcak uses satellite photography and software to search for geometries in the Egyptian desert that suggest buried buildings and ruins. Using remote sensing, she has found several pyramids and thousands of tombs and settlement sites; her images of the city of Tanis, in the Nile Delta, have revealed large areas of the city that were unknown, despite excavation having taken place there since the nineteenth century.[4]

El Dorado and Atlantis

Were cities such as El Dorado and Atlantis purely imaginary, or were they part real, part legend, evolving into something different in the process of the telling? Like the tale of the fish that got away, getting bigger and bigger each time the story is told, the legend of El Dorado, the city made of gold, sounds like an expansion of the tales told by the Spanish conquistadors of ancient cities merely rich in gold and silver, not made of it. And so it was. The story began as that of *El Hombre Dorado* (the Golden Man), the descriptive used by Spanish observers who described the initiation ceremonies of a chieftain carried out by the Muisca people (*c.*600–1600) in what is now Colombia. The rites involved the new chieftain covering himself in gold dust:

> At this time, they stripped the heir to his skin, and anointed him with a sticky earth on which they placed gold dust so that he was completely covered with this metal. They placed him on the raft ... and at his feet they placed a great heap of gold and emeralds for him to offer to his god.[5]

This story and name was conflated with a search, during the late sixteenth century, for a city of gold called Manõa, which was said to be on the shores of the legendary Lake Parime. On his deathbed, a captain called Juan Martinez, part of the expedition led by Diego de Ordaz around 1520, described having come upon Manõa while lost, and spending seven months there. His account prompted Sir Walter Raleigh to become one of many adventurers to search for this mythical city.[6] The last explorations were still taking place in the nineteenth century. There was gold in great quantities in Central and South America, quantities that seemed unbelievable in Europe, and these stories, written in letters or passed orally from man to man until they returned to Spain, helped to encourage funding of further expeditions. Tales about cities of gold also raised the status of the speaker in the eyes of his stay-at-home fellow countrymen, and it is not difficult to see how they might have been embellished and augmented until explorers imagined an entire city paved with gold bricks.

Another famous lost city, Atlantis, began its existence as an allegory in Plato's dialogues *Timaeus* and the unfinished *Critias* (*c.*360 BC) about the hubris of nation-states – but that has not stopped people from searching for an actual place. The fuller description is in the *Timaeus,* in which is told the story of the island nation that lost its god-like element over many generations and eventually fought a war with Athens, whose people refused to accept being enslaved by the Atlanteans. Athens won, and after a day and night of earthquakes and floods, the island of Atlantis sunk into the sea, never to be seen again.

Given the allegorical nature of so much of Plato's writing, there is little reason to think that Atlantis refers to a real place.

Thomas Cole, *The Consummation of Empire*, 1835–6, oil on canvas, 130.2 × 193 cm (51¹/₄ × 76 in), New York Historical Society; the fifth and last work in his *The Course of Empire* series

Nevertheless, its story has captured the imagination of many writers and others, including no less than Thomas More and Francis Bacon in the sixteenth and seventeenth centuries, while a nineteenth-century scholar, Ignatius L. Donnelly, helped to popularize the myth in his *Atlantis: The Antediluvian World* (1882), which misconstrued Plato's writing as a literal historical account. The public had already been encouraged to believe that Atlantis was a real, lost city when it featured in Jules Verne's hugely popular 1870 novel, *Ten Thousand Leagues Under the Sea*.

Plato's Atlantis may not have existed, but there have been cities swallowed by the sea, buried by earthquake, volcanic eruption or rising waters. In 2015, the Hellenic Ministry of Culture announced the discovery of an Early Bronze Age (third millennium BC) city off the coast of Greece in Khilada Bay, south of Athens, covering 12 acres (5 hectares).[7] It includes what seem to be fortifications with curved towers, a feature not seen in other sites of this period. Could it be that Plato's allegory was inspired by a city like this, once present and then lost long before his time?[8]

LOST STRUCTURES

Just as whole cities might well be lost to jungle, lava or sea, and small seeds of truth may germinate into vast settlements, so individual buildings or structures that inhabit the realm of mythical history might grow from oral tradition, watered by time until they develop into legend, hardened through repetition into fact, then relegated once again to myth for lack of evidence.

The Labyrinth at Knossos

A Greek myth tells of the Minotaur, half-man, half-bull, who was the offspring of Pasiphaë, wife of King Minos, and Zeus, who seduced the queen in the form of a white bull. Partly out of shame, partly pragmatically, Minos imprisoned the Minotaur in a labyrinth designed by the inventor Daedalus. Every seven years, the finest youths and maidens of Athens were sent to Crete as tribute, condemned to enter the labyrinth and become food for the Minotaur. That is, until the Athenian prince Theseus was given a thread by the Cretan princess Ariadne to unwind as he walked through the labyrinth, so that after having slain the Minotaur he was able to find his way out again.

The Bronze Age palace at Knossos was discovered at the end of the nineteenth century, and systematic excavation by the British archaeologist Sir Arthur Evans began in 1900.[9]

Reconstructed stairways in part of the Bronze Age palace at Knossos, second millennium BC; the many levels and dark corridors of the palace seemed labyrinthine to its twentieth-century excavators

The elaborate warren of corridors and rooms he uncovered, which could reasonably be described as 'labyrinthine', led him to conclude that the palace itself was the labyrinth of legend. More than half a million tourists visit Knossos every year, but it is no longer the only candidate for the Minotaur's lair.

In 2009, a team of archaeologists began to explore an ancient stone quarry on the south side of Crete near Gortyn, the ancient Roman capital of the island.[10] The quarry is riddled with tunnels, 4 kilometres (2.5 miles) of them, which some think make up a more compelling site for the mythical labyrinth than the Bronze Age palace. Long called the 'Labyrinthos Caves', they were believed by tourists from the twelfth to the nineteenth centuries to be the site of the Minotaur legend. This was before the discovery of the ruins of Knossos, however, which became a magnet for tourism, especially after the elaborate reconstructions there financed by Evans. Gortyn or Knossos? Each claims association with a place of legend that may have indeed been lost and now found, or may never have existed at all.

The Hanging Gardens of Babylon

Because there are no known Babylonian texts that refer to the Hanging Gardens of Babylon, now in modern Iraq, it is thought that their existence may be legendary.[11] Nebuchadnezzar II (reigned c.605–562 BC) was meant to have built the gardens for his wife, Queen Amytis, who missed the green landscape of her home in Media (northern Iran). Classical writers in the first century BC and first century AD, including Quintus Curtius Rufus, Diodorus Siculus and Strabo, do describe the gardens, but it is not clear if any actually saw them.

Diodorus Siculus (c.90–30 BC) offered the most elaborate description in his *Bibliotheca Historia* ('Historical Library', c.50 BC), stating that the gardens were around 400 Greek feet on each side, 'sloped like a hillside and the several parts of the structure rose from one another, tier on tier, the appearance of the whole resembling a theatre'. The highest tier was 'level with the circuit wall of the battlements of the city'. The walls were twenty-two Greek feet thick, with walkways ten feet wide. The structure, meant to hold soil and moisture, he describes as made initially of brick bonded with cement, then a layer of bitumen, then a layer of lead 'to the end that the moisture from the soil might not penetrate beneath'; all of this was then piled with soil and 'thickly planted with trees of every kind that, by their great size or other charm, could give pleasure to the beholder'. This level of detail suggests the description of a real place, though Diodorus wrote that a Syrian king built it. Quintus Curtius Rufus, writing in the first century AD, describes a structure similar enough to grant further credence to its one-time existence.

Recent scholarship suggests that the Babylonian gardens might have been conflated with gardens that did exist, built by Assyrian king Sennacherib (704–681 BC) in Nineveh, some 160 kilometres (100 miles) to the north of Babylon. The fifth-century BC historian Herodotus does not mention the Hanging Gardens when describing Babylon, which is a conspicuous oversight if they actually existed there. Archaeologists have found an 80-kilometre (50-mile) network of waterways, comprising aqueducts, canals and dams, which carried water to Nineveh, along with a series of water-raising screws that could have raised the water uphill to irrigate the gardens.[12]

Imaginary reconstruction of the Hanging Gardens of Babylon, ninteenth century, hand-coloured woodcut

If the famous Hanging Gardens were actually the ones in Nineveh, they do not qualify as lost at all – their remnants can be visited today. If there was a similar garden in Babylon, it might have been damaged, destroyed or its materials reused over the millennia of invaders, including the Assyrians. The picture grows more intriguing, as it was King Sennacherib who ordered the destruction of the defensive walls, palaces and temples of Babylon in 689 BC, as a deterrent to the regular uprising of the population against their Assyrian conquerors. If they ever existed in Babylon, it may have been then that the gardens met their fate – possibly to be reconstructed in Nineveh, maybe even with elements dismantled and transferred to the Assyrian capital.

The Court of King Arthur at Camelot

Another site-specific legend concerns the mythical-historical kingdom of King Arthur of Britain, whose court at Camelot may, or may not, have been real. Some have associated his legend with the story of Alfred the Great, who as king of Wessex from AD 871 to 899 defended it against Saxon invaders. While King Arthur's story inspired medieval romances, most famously *Le Morte d'Arthur* by Sir Thomas Malory (1485), there are far older

Medieval reconstruction of the Round Table of Camelot, Winchester Castle; the object has been displayed for centuries in the Great Hall, painted with the names and positions around the table of King Arthur and his twenty-four knights

sources that mention him, including the medieval Welsh poem *Y Gododdin*, the tenth-century *Annales Cambriae (Annals of Wales)*, the twelfth-century *Life of St Gildas* by Caradoc of Llancarfan, and the *Historia Brittonum* (*History of the Britons*, written around AD 828). The last is the earliest surviving text to tell of Arthur, and it does so with sufficient detail (specifying twelve battles won by Arthur, who is described as a *dux bellorum* – a military general, rather than a king) to suggest it is real history, or was believed to be and was recorded as such. The truth is probably a hybrid of scraps of fact embellished over time. For instance, the *Historia Brittonum* specifies that at the last of the twelve battles, the Battle of Badon, Arthur single-handedly killed 960 men, which sounds unlikely.

Arthur's story is integral to English national pride, and there have been many candidates proposed for Arthur's court, called Camelot. Sir Thomas Malory specifies that Camelot was at Winchester, in southern England, but it remains unclear how much of Malory's story was faithful penning of spoken legend, and how much was new fictions he developed based on those legends. Tintagel Castle in Cornwall is another pretender, though its current, romantic incarnation is a thirteenth-century structure as well; by all accounts, Arthur was active in the early sixth century. A relic of Arthuriana, supposedly the Round Table of his knightly court, hangs in Winchester Castle (it has been dated by dendrochronology to the thirteenth century), and another Round Table hangs on the wall of Chartres Cathedral, in France. The desire to find physical evidence to prove mythical history is actually history proper may inspire anachronistic thinking, or the forcing of sites, objects, graves, bones and the like to stand in for missing originals that may have never existed. Regarding Camelot, 'At this stage of the enquiry, one can only say that there may well have been a historical Arthur ... but the historian can, as yet, say nothing of value about him.'[13]

LOST RELICS

The same might be said for lost relics. There was a lively trade in relics throughout the Middle Ages, particularly stimulated by the Crusades from the end of the eleventh century to the end of the thirteenth. A return from the Holy Land offered plausible provenances for bits of bone that may, or may not, have belonged to historical saints (who may, or may not, have existed, and who may, or may not, have fit the description offered by the thirteenth-century *Golden Legend,* the group biography of the saints). Throughout this time and afterwards there was concern over the authenticity of relics: the Shroud of Turin, brought back from the Holy Land around 1353 by a French knight called Geoffrey de Charney was already dismissed by Bishop Pierre d'Arcis as a forgery in 1390. That did not stop the pilgrims, however, nor have they been dissuaded by four separate, objective laboratory tests undertaken in recent decades, all of which show that the image on the shroud is a medieval painting. Faith and a desire to find tangible evidence of one's belief are stronger than fact.[14]

Religious Relics

To include Christian relics in a chapter entitled 'Lost, or Never Was?' invites polemic. But much Biblical description is unclear, clearly exaggerated, or poetic to the point that extracting specifics can be a challenge, and this often applies to physical relics. Numbers 1:45–6, for instance, states that the Israelites had an army comprising 603,000 men twenty or older – and this, during the sojourn in the wilderness, when sustaining even a fraction of that number would have been extremely difficult. It is assumed that these extremely large numbers in the Bible are rhetorical devices meaning 'a lot', rather than an attempt at numerical accuracy.

The Holy Grail, the cup from which Christ is believed to have drunk at the Last Supper, and/or which was used to catch some of his blood as he hung upon the cross, is an invention of medieval romances, with the first known written reference coming as late as 1190, in the fictional epic *Perceval, le Conte du Graal* by Chrétien de Troyes. Indeed, the Grail is more of a presence in pagan Celtic mythology than in anything Christian.[15] There is no mention of it in primary source material (the Biblical stories of the life of Jesus, and the Apocrypha written within the first two centuries AD). On the other hand, there was doubtlessly a real person named Jesus of Nazareth who was executed by the Romans in Judaea, and as an observant Jew, the historical Jesus would have had a cup out of which he drank at the Passover *seder*, the ritual feast that celebrates the freeing of the Israelites from slavery in Egypt; and so, logically, if such an object existed, it is lost but might, conceivably, be found. Nevertheless, and despite *Da Vinci Code*-induced enthusiasm for the Holy Grail as a metaphor for Mary Magdalene or the offspring of Mary Magdalene and Jesus, the hunt for a physical cup makes little sense.

Jewish relics include those from the Temple of Herod in Jerusalem (the so-called Second Temple, built by the Jews following their return from captivity in Babylon), sacked in AD 70 by a Roman force led by Titus (son of the emperor Vespasian) during the First Jewish War (AD 66–73). Spoils from the looting of the temple were used to help finance the rebuilding of Rome after the Great Fire of AD 64, and the erection of the Flavian amphitheatre, or Colosseum.[16] Ezra 1:5–10 says that the Jews were allowed to return to Israel from Babylon with some of the gold and silver that had been taken by Nebuchadnezzar's armies when the first temple was destroyed in 586 BC, and during the four centuries of its existence, the Second Temple's treasury must have grown with the gifts and dedications of worshippers, along with obligatory temple tributes. Cicero wrote of influxes of gold and silver into Jerusalem during his lifetime.[17] Jewish tradition says that there was so much precious metal in the temple that when it was burned, the gold and silver melted and ran down into the cracks between the stones. Roman soldiers then dismantled the building stone by stone to retrieve the metal. The triumphal Arch of Titus and Vespasian in Rome includes a relief (see chapter 2) showing soldiers carrying plunder from the temple, including a great menorah and trumpets, but apart from these images, what exactly was in the vast treasure brought back to Rome is unknown.

Secular Relics

Secular relics of great men may also be misted over through time. Vasari describes a shield made of wood from a fig tree, painted by a young Leonardo da Vinci (1452–1519) with a monster inspired by Medusa:

> He began to think what he could paint upon it, that might be able to terrify all who should come upon it, producing the same effect as once did the head of Medusa. For this purpose, then, Leonardo carried to a room of his own, into which no one entered save himself, lizards great and small, crickets, serpents, butterflies, grasshoppers, bats and other strange kids of such-like animals (some of which he dissected), out of which he formed a great, ugly creature, most horrible and terrifying, which emitted a poisonous breath and turned the air to flame; and he made it coming out of a dark and jagged rock, belching forth venom from its open throat, fire from its eyes, and smoke from its nostrils, in so strange a fashion that it appeared altogether a monstrous and horrible thing. So long did he labour over making it, that the stench of the dead animals in the room was past bearing, but Leonardo did not notice it, so great was the love that he bore towards art.[18]

Unknown Flemish artist, after Leonardo da Vinci, *Medusa's Head*, 1600, oil on canvas, 49 × 74 cm (19¹/₂ × 29 in), Galleria degli Uffizi, Florence

Caravaggio, *Shield with Medusa's Head*, 1597, oil on canvas mounted on wood, 60 × 55 cm (23¹/₂ × 21¹/₂ in), Galleria degli Uffizi, Florence

This lost work is usually referred to as the *Medusa Shield*, but from the description it appears to be a hybrid monster instead. Nevertheless, it inspired numerous artists to try their hands at a similar subject, most famously Caravaggio, who painted two versions, in 1596 and 1597.

The vividness and specificity of Vasari's language suggests that what he was describing was real. In trying to separate legendary products of imagination and oral tradition from descriptions of objects that once existed but have been lost, the level of specificity is key, as is the 'provenance' of the story. Although Vasari was only eight years old when Leonardo died, he lived most of his life in Florence and knew many people who had known Leonardo personally. It is likely that the stories of

Leonardo's life are but one step removed from someone who knew the artist, and could be corroborated by others who also knew him. Vasari's research technique of writing to family members and gathering stories that, in this case, were only a few decades old, also lends credence to his description. Contrast this, for instance, to Plato's description of Atlantis from the *Timaeus*:

> The island was larger than Libya and Asia put together ...
> In this island of Atlantis there was a great and wonderful empire which had rule over the whole island and several others, and over parts of the continent and, furthermore, the men of Atlantis had subjected the parts of Libya within the columns of Hercules as far as Egypt and of Europe as far as Tyrrhenia.

This great power from the Atlantic attacked Athens, but was repulsed. As punishment meted out by the gods,

> There occurred violent earthquakes and floods; and in a single day and night of misfortune all your war-like men, in a body, sank into the earth, and the island of Atlantis, in like manner, disappeared into the depths of the sea.

And this was meant to have happened 'nine thousand years ago'. Plato's description seems quite obviously invented, a means of making his allegorical point. It makes one wonder at the very idea that explorers and historians have taken Plato's text as a description of a real place.

The Three Sacred Treasures of Japan

The Imperial Regalia of Japan, also called the Three Sacred Treasures of Japan, are said to include a mirror called Yata no Kagami (representing the virtue of wisdom), a sword called Kusanagi (valour) and a jewel called Yasakani no Magatama (benevolence). But whether or not these treasures exist is an open question, and possibly a matter of faith.

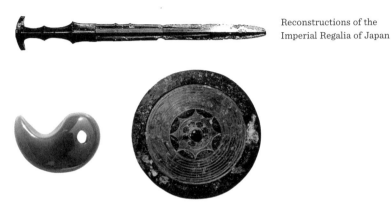

Reconstructions of the Imperial Regalia of Japan

Dating back to AD 690, these items are traditionally presented to the emperors of Japan by priests during coronation ceremonies. Tradition also says that they were brought down to Earth by the ancestor of the Japanese imperial line, Ninigi-no-Mikoto, the armaments given to him by his grandmother, goddess of the sun, Amaterasu, who sent him down from the heavens to bring peace to warring Japan. Each of the treasures has its own story. Amaterasu was said to have hidden from her brother, Susanoo-no-Mikoto, taking shelter in a cave and causing the world to grow dark. The goddess Ame-no-Uzume-no-Mikoto hung the mirror and the jewel outside the cave's entrance as a trick to draw her out. Amaterasu saw her reflection in the mirror and was startled long enough for the gods to pull her from the cave. To apologize for having driven his sister into hiding, Susanoo presented her with the sword, which he had acquired from an eight-headed serpent called Yamata no Orochi. The first emperor of Japan, Jimmu, Ninigi's great-grandson, was said to have inherited the Treasures from him. They were the physical manifestation of the legitimacy and lineage of the ruler who possessed them.[19]

There are stories of the treasures having been lost and found, stories that shift depending on who is telling them, and so the truth is evasive. A battle was fought on the Kanmom Straits in 1185, when the emperor at the time, Antoku, was only eight. To avoid capture, his grandmother threw the emperor, the Sacred Treasures and herself out of the boat and into the sea. The mirror was recovered, but an enemy soldier who tried to force open the box in which it was contained was struck blind. The jewel was later found by divers, but the sword remained lost. Some say that a new sword was forged then, others that a decoy had been thrown into the water, yet others that the sword rose out of the sea and returned to its shrine through supernatural means. Whatever the fate of the original, or subsequently rendered versions of the Sacred Treasures, they have retained their symbolic power. It is said that when it was clear that Japan would lose the Second World War, among his final orders, Emperor Hirohito instructed the Lord Keeper of the Privy Seal of Japan to defend the Treasures at all costs.[20]

It is forbidden for the public to see the Treasures, so their very existence cannot be proven; they are revealed only to the emperor and selected priests. What was said to be two of the treasures (the jewel and the sword) were displayed at the accession of Emperor Akihito in 1989 and his enthronement in 1990, but were wrapped in shrouds. Popular belief holds that the three are safeguarded in separate shrines: Ise Grand Shrine in the Mie Prefecture holds the mirror, Atsuta Shrine in Nagoya holds the sword (or its replica), and Three Palaces Sanctuaries in Tokyo keeps the jewel. Whether or not you believe that these Treasures came from the gods, were lost at sea and found again, still exist today, or are more symbolic than literal, is largely a matter of faith.

—

Was this chieftain Priam? Was this city Sacred Ilios? No one will ever fathom the question, whether these were the names which men used when the celebrated king still looked out from his elevated fortress over the Trojan Plain to the Hellespont. Perhaps these names are the poet's invention. Who can know? ... But now, under our eyes, this site has again been disclosed.[21]

Many writers attempted to assign a known ruin to Troy, and in 1822, Charles Maclaren identified the hill of Hisarlik, on the Turkish mainland opposite the tip of the Gallipoli Peninsula, as the most likely site; Frank Calvert, an English consular official and amateur archaeologist, began exploring the mound in 1864, having bought the farmland that surrounded it some years earlier. The soon-to-be-famous discoverer of Troy, German businessman Heinrich Schliemann, had searched for remains at other possible sites, unsuccessfully, and was convinced by Calvert that this was the right spot. He received permission to excavate the site and began in 1871. In 1873, Schliemann announced that he had found what he called the Scaean Gate, which he specified as the one that Homer described. He wrote: 'I have proven that, in remote antiquity, there was in the plain of Troy a large city, destroyed of old by a fearful catastrophe... consequently, this city answers perfectly to the Homeric description...'[22] But does it?

The discovery of Troy was extraordinary but complicated. There was not one lost city but several successive cities, dating from the Bronze Age through the Roman period – from around 3000 BC to AD 500. Schliemann was convinced that Level II, near the bottom of the mound, was the city attacked by the Greeks, and the rich gold remains found here he called 'Priam's Treasure', after the king of Troy. Schliemann's discovery finally removed Troy from the realm of mythical history into the empirically defined zone of history proper. What was once believed to be a true, then dismissed as legend, had now been confirmed, this time by hard evidence. But that was not the end of the story.

The methods by which Schliemann excavated the mound at Hisarlik have been condemned by scholars ever since as having caused irreparable damage to the site, destroying as much or more than it recovered. One archaeologist even joked that Schliemann did to Troy what the Greeks had failed to do during their siege – levelled the city walls.[23] And despite his claims for Level II, it was unclear which of the many ancient cities found in layers on the site was the Troy of the Homeric epics (if indeed that Troy ever existed). The site was real enough, but did it prove the stories? Later archaeologists, with a subtler hand and more experience than Schliemann, discerned nine cities in the layers of the hill, in forty-seven separate strata.[24] The German architect-archaeologist Wilhelm Dörpfeld, who worked with Schliemann at Troy, found archaeological evidence for the destruction of the city in the layer called Troy VI, as well as a defensive ditch that may have surrounded the external walls of the city. He was convinced that this level, dating to around 1250 BC, was the Bronze Age city of Troy. However, in excavations carried out by Carl Blegen from 1932 to 1938, it became clear that Troy VI was probably levelled by an earthquake, not an army. The lack of arrowheads and other weapons made a battle here unlikely. Blegen suggested instead that the remains in level VIIa comprised the best evidence for the site of a war, with evidence of extensive burning on both the stones and skeletons found there; the layer is dated to c.1184 BC.[25]

Contemporary engraving showing excavations at Hisarlik in June 1873; from Heinrich Schliemann, *Ilios, ville et pays des Troyens: Fouilles de 1871 á 1882* (Paris, 1885)

Troy was made a UNESCO World Heritage site in 1998, and it continues to be excavated, despite the damage done by Schliemann. The mysteries inherent in it continued, however, until as recently as 1993. The gold horde that Schliemann called 'Priam's Treasure' included a pair of gold diadems (the 'Jewels of Helen'), 8,750 gold rings, and scores of other items made of gold, silver, copper and electrum (an alloy of gold and silver). Schliemann smuggled the hoard out of Turkey in his personal effects and had his wife photographed wearing much of the jewellery. Most of this collection eventually went to the Royal Museums of Berlin, though Schliemann did return some items to the Ottoman government in exchange for permission to return to Troy to dig further. The haul was recovered from the level associated with Troy II, and therefore predates by centuries the layer of Troy that was most likely ruled by Priam, Homer's ruler of Troy.

The Treasure was hidden underneath the Berlin Zoo in 1945, then disappeared. It was assumed that if it still existed at all, it must have been carried off by the Red Army when Berlin fell.

Left: Photograph of Sophia Schliemann wearing the so-called Treasure of Priam, c.1874
Right: Some of the objects comprising the Treasure of Priam

For almost half a century the Soviet Union denied knowing anything the jewels – until in September 1993 they were identified in the stores of Moscow's Pushkin Museum.[26] The horde was lost for millennia, then excavated and misidentified as 'Priam's Treasure', smuggled abroad, hidden by the Nazis, looted by the Red Army and lost once again to the rest of the world while held by the Soviets. A protracted plan to return the treasure to Germany (the Turkish government, which arguable has prior claim, has not yet weighed in) has been blocked by Russian museum officials, who consider the looted art compensation for the vast damage, in goods and lives, wrought by the Nazis; in confirmation, legislation was passed in Russia in 1998 legalizing Russian looting from Germany during the Second World War.[27]

CONCLUSION

LOST IS JUST ANOTHER WORD
FOR WAITING TO BE FOUND

Off Rozel Point on the shore of the Great Salt Lake in Utah,
a masterpiece by sculptor Robert Smithson (1938–73) is slowly
vanishing. Spiral Jetty was built in 1970 of earth, water, the salt
crystals that dust the lake like snowfall, and 6,650 tons of local
basalt rock. From the sky, it resembles the tendril of a fern, or
a bishop's mitre. Some 460 metres (1,500 ft) long and 4.6 metres
(15 ft) wide, it was never meant to last forever. When wind, rain
and erosion have completed their work on his piece of land art,
it will disappear. Regular intervention could maintain it, but
that was not Smithson's wish.[1] By 1999, when Spiral Jetty was
donated by Smithson's estate to the Dia Art Foundation, this
work of art was lost. The waters of the lake had risen, and the
rock and earth from which it was built had eroded to the point
that it was submerged. A few years later the waters receded, and
it re-emerged after almost thirty years. Lost art found – only to
be lost again. Smithson wanted nature to run its course. When it
was ready to swallow or disperse his sculpture, so it should be.

Robert Smithson, *Spiral Jetty*, 1970, basalt rock, salt crystals, earth and water, L: 457 m
(1,500 ft), Rozal Point, Great Salt Lake, Utah

IS SOME LOST ART BETTER OFF LOST?

In his will, Franz Kafka (1883–1924) stated his wish that all of his unpublished writings should be burned after his death. His friend and literary executor, Max Brod, did Kafka a great wrong, and the world a great right, in refusing to follow through with this nihilistic request. Brod rationalized his decision by saying that he had told Kafka that he would not carry out this wish. That Kafka did not then choose a different literary executor suggested to Brod that he did not really want his writings destroyed. Books considered literary masterpieces, including *The Trial, The Castle* and *Amerika,* were among those published posthumously, thanks to Brod. There are many more stories that are yet to be published, and not just from the works administered by Brod. In 1933, the German Gestapo seized some twenty notebooks from Kafka's lover, Dora Diamant.[2] They may have been destroyed, but there remains a chance that these lost writings will turn up. Lost books do.

A lost 1852 novella by the American poet Walt Whitman, called *The Life and Adventures of Jack Engle,* was discovered in 2016 by a graduate student. It seems that Whitman wished to have his early writing forgotten: 'My serious wish were to have all those crude and boyish pieced quietly dropp'd in oblivion.'[3] In 2015, a novel by Harper Lee, *Go Set a Watchman,* written in 1957, was published to much controversy. The author of *To Kill a Mockingbird* had been clear that she did not wish to publish another novel, and had held back this one, which also features Atticus Finch, the hero of *To Kill a Mockingbird.* The novel was rediscovered in 2011 by Lee's lawyer, tucked away in a safety deposit box. Lee may have been suffering from dementia at the time (she died in 2016), and it is not clear whether she was genuinely keen to publish or if she was being taken advantage of by her lawyer.[4] The novel, while a bestseller, was critically panned and negatively impacted Lee's reputation as an author, among both critics and fans. The publication of Kafka's nearly lost works, which he claimed to wish disposed of, elevated him into the literary stratosphere. In Lee's case, some might say that her legacy would have been better served had her lost novel stayed lost.

CAN LOST ART BE REPLICATED?

Technology today is such that, in many cases, we can create a new version of what has been lost, or indeed what might have been but never was. The Next Rembrandt project[5] is a collaboration between a team at the Delft University of Technology, the Mauritshuis in The Hague, the Rembrandt House Museum in Amsterdam and Microsoft to create a digitally printed painting in the style of Rembrandt; the portrait's face is fictional, based on a facial recognition algorithm and computer hybridization of real Rembrandt subjects. The result was unveiled in Amsterdam in April 2016 and thoroughly impressed art critics and art historians. The Next Rembrandt project website opens with the line, 'Can a great master be brought back to create one more painting?' It appears so. This act of creating an imaginary artwork could also easily be applied to works that are lost. One could imagine an entire museum of them, the realization of each work based on surviving descriptions, copies or photographs, and then printed in two

Rembrandt-style portrait created by The Next Rembrandt project, 2016, digital print; the painting was created using deep learning algorithms and facial recognition techniques, and comprises more than 148 million pixels, based on 168,263 painting fragments from Rembrandt's complete body of work

Morehshin Allahyari, *King Uthal*, 2015, 3D-printed plastic and electrical components, 30.5 × 10.2 x 8.9 cm (12 × 4 × 3.5 in), from her series *Material Speculation: ISIS*

or three dimensions to the closest approximation of what the original probably looked like.

Bringing lost art back to life has moved from science fiction to fact. In 2017, Iranian-American artist Morehshin Allahyari exhibited twelve 3D-printed artefacts destroyed by ISIS, including a Roman-period statue of King Uthal of Hatra, in a show called *She Who Sees the Unknown*, exhibiting her *Material Speculation* series.[6] In April 2016, a 3D-printed, two-thirds scale replica of the Arch of Triumph at Palmyra, also destroyed by ISIS, was raised in London's Trafalgar Square before travelling to cities around the world.[7] Madrid-based firm Factum Arte specializes in museum-quality 3D scanning of art and artefacts, archiving extremely detailed, high-quality digital images of objects that may deteriorate. These can also be printed, sometimes in authentic materials, for museum exhibition. The firm created a crevice-by-crevice rendering of the tomb of King Tutankhamun, and a full-sized replica of Lenin's tomb, including his 3D-printed embalmed body, is planned for exhibition at the 2017 Venice Biennale, and they are producing selected lost paintings for a television series. One can imagine, in the near future, a physical museum of lost art, hung with printed replicas

Arch of Triumph from Palmyra, destroyed in 2015, as erected in Trafalgar Square, London, April 2016, H: 6 m (20 ft); the original arch was built in the first century AD

– Las Vegas, with its copies of the Venetian Doge's Palace and the Eiffel Tower, seems the likeliest location.

Any such work will necessarily be a mechanical production or reproduction, the digital creation of a computer programmed by technologists. The humanity or soul with which an artist imbues his or her handcrafted work cannot be replicated. The idea that original, handmade art contains the soul and passion of the artist, using the object as a medium of human-to-human communication, has been a part of the discussion about art for centuries. While newly created works can be artificially aged, as forgers are wont to do to their fresh handiwork, that patina of history, the way that an object wears its biography in cracks and creases, *craquelure* and fading, cannot authentically be replicated. A museum of lost art, like the models of the tomb of Tutankhamun in the Valley of the Kings or the replica of Lascaux Cave in France, would be of immense aesthetic, historical and intellectual interest, but it would not replace the real thing. It would be without a soul.

LOSSES THAT FALL BETWEEN THE CRACKS

The stories told in this book have been categorized based on how the art was lost, but there are countless works that fall between the cracks, or the fate of which remains unknown. Richard Serra's 1981 *Tilted Arc* was commissioned for the plaza in front of the Jacob K. Javits Federal Building in Manhattan, as part of the federal Arts in Architecture programme. But the COR-ten steel ribbon, 37 metres (120 ft) long and x 3.7 metres (12 ft) tall, was considered by many to be an imposition, requiring pedestrians to take a long tilted arc path around the sculpture, rather than simply crossing the plaza directly. It was removed in 1989 at the end of a high-profile trial in which Serra (b.1938) argued that *Tilted Arc's* location was integral to its meaning, and that it could not exist if it were moved elsewhere. At a 1985 public hearing to discuss the issue, 122 people testified in favour of the work and 58 against it; those in favour included artists Claes Oldenburg, Keith Haring and Philip Glass. It was a landmark case of artists arguing in court in support of another

Richard Serra, *Tilted Arc*, 1981, steel, 3.7 × 36.5 m (12 × 120 ft), Federal Plaza, New York City; whereabouts unknown

artist's work, with an air of the death penalty about it – the death of an artwork. A five-person jury voted 4–1 to remove the sculpture and, after an appeal, it was dismantled. It is said to be in storage, with the artist wishing it never be displayed again.[8]

Another mysterious story of loss involves a famous samurai sword (*katana*) made by the great Japanese sword smith Gorō Nyūdoō Masamune (1264–1343). The so-called *Honjō Masamune*, described as one of the finest swords ever made, takes its name from one of its samurai wielders, General Honjō Shigenaga (1540–1614), who served under Daimyō (Lord) Uesugi Kenshin. According to the story, Honjō was attacked by another samurai, Umanosuke, who was in possession of the *Honjo Masamune*. During the fight, Umanosuke split Honjō's helmet in two with the sword, but Honjō won, taking *Honjō Masamume* as a trophy and carrying it until around 1595, when he sold the sword to Toyotomi Hidetsugu.[9] From there the blade passed through numerous hands until it ended up in the hands of the Tokugawa shoguns, who ruled Japan as the last feudal military government in what is called the Edo Period (1600–1868). Its last known owner was Tokugawa Iemasa (1884–1963). It was classified as a National Treasure of Japan in 1939.

A fragmented and suspect story of its fate states that in December 1945, following the defeat of Japan and the end of the Second World War, Tokugawa Iemasa brought the *Honjō Masamune* and the rest of his sword collection, fifteen blades in all, to the police station in Mejiro, a district in Tokyo. They remained there until January 1946, when the police handed over the swords to someone who appeared to be an Allied officer, identified as 'Sgt. Coldy Bimore'. This sounds like a phonetic spelling of something like 'Cody Bilmore', though there is no record of anyone with a name approximating this among Allied officers stationed in Japan at the time. He was ostensibly from the Foreign Liquidations Commission of the Army Forces of the Western Pacific, but there is no reason to believe that this was the man's real identity, and it is not clear why the police would hand over such treasures. Nevertheless, none of the swords has been seen again.[10]

Innumerable other artworks are no more than descriptions in the history books, or copies of uncertain authenticity. The *Herakles* and *Apoxyomenos* by Lysippos. The *Athena Lemnia* by Phidias and the *Aphrodite of Knidos* by Praxiteles. The final section of the *Bayeux Tapestry*. Four panels of Duccio's *Maestà* altarpiece. Jan van Eyck's *Woman Bathing* or *Yeper Madonna* or *Lomellini Triptych*. There are endless works of lost art, far more than have survived, far more than fills the thousands of museums the world over, the hundreds of thousands of churches and temples, the millions of homes. Each has a story, but to tell every one would mean a book without end. Consider the lost works of a single artist, sixteenth-century sculptor and goldsmith Benvenuto Cellini (1500–71): a gold chalice and a golden morse (the clasp used to attach a cape) for Pope Clement VII; large-scale silver statues of Mars, Vulcan and Jupiter, made for François I during a time in Paris; the gilded cover of a prayer book offered as a gift from Pope Paul III to Holy Roman Emperor Charles V; a silver chalice made for the cardinal of Ferrara; a bust of Julius Caesar. Because Cellini often worked in precious metals, these objects were in particular danger of being melted down. The gold and silver in the Papal collection may have been lost when Pope Pius VI, having yielded to Napoleon's army in 1797, was obliged to pay a cease-fire fee of 30 million francs. The terms of the treaty dictated that one third of this sum could be paid in 'plate and jewels', which almost certainly included dozens of works of the gold and silversmiths' art.

Many losses are forestalled by the miracle workers who are modern art conservators. In 2002, at New York's Metropolitan Museum of Art, the wooden plinth supporting a life-sized *Adam* (early 1490s) by Renaissance sculptor Tullio Lombardo (*c.*1455–1532) collapsed, bringing Adam down with it. The marble statue shattered into hundreds of splinters, along with twenty-eight more significant chunks. It was a disaster, but for Met marble conservators, it was also a fascinating puzzle – putting Humpty Dumpty back together again in an exercise akin to a three-dimensional jigsaw puzzle. It took a dozen years, a team of more than a dozen specialists, and even a trip to the hospital for the marble 'patient' to undergo a CT scan. The result was so successful that the museum exhibited the repaired artwork in 2013–14 alongside videos showing the behind-the-scenes process of research and conservation. Sometimes the brilliance of conservators can save lost art, coaxing works wounded beyond recognition back to life.

CAUSE FOR OPTIMISM

Among the various categories of lost art, there are some works that must be considered gone forever. There is the slimmest of chances, for instance, that a work from the Dresden Gemäldegalerie survived the Allied fire bombings of February 1945, was swept up by a soldier or citizen and squirrelled away all these years, mislaid or hidden but still intact. Objects destroyed by their owner or creator, temporal works, and destroyed in acts of iconoclasm must likewise be bid farewell.

Nevertheless, there are some categories of lost art that allow optimism. Theft, above all, offers hope, as even thieves know that their stolen objects are of high value only if they are preserved. Police tend not to take seriously any threat to knowingly destroy an artwork if, for instance, a ransom goes unpaid, because unlike a kidnap victim, the artwork cannot tattle on the thieves if it is recovered, and obliterating the object renders it valueless – it's like setting fire to a bag full of cash, benefiting no one. Theft is always preferable to damage or destruction, because at least the object exists and may be found again. It happened as recently as the summer of 2017, when the owners of a New Mexico furniture and antiques shop bought a painting as part of an estate sale. When several customers asked if it was a work by Willem de Kooning, they did some research and soon suspected that the painting was *Woman-Ochre* (1954–5), which had been stolen from the University of Arizona Museum of Art in 1985. It had hung in a suburban bedroom in a cheap gold frame for thirty years. Valued at more than 100 million dollars, it is now back on display at the museum.[11]

That we do not simply shrug and move on when we learn of a lost masterpiece is a testament to the love felt for art, the sense that it is greater than ourselves, whether we are driven to protect and maintain it through interest in its financial value alone or its cultural importance or its beauty. People have died trying to defend or recover art. Soldiers stood in breathless determination inside the darkened hull of St Bavo's Cathedral in Ghent while Protestant rioters raged outside in 1566, ready to defend van Eyck's *Adoration of the Mystic Lamb* with their lives against the threat of its being dragged out of the cathedral and immolated in the square by those who condemned it as an icon of Catholicism. Alcazar staff ran back into the burning castle to hurl works like Velázquez's *Las Meninas* out the window to safety, risking suffocation and flames. The Monuments Men of the Second World War sought to rescue inanimate objects, bits of stone and wood and canvas, while an estimated 60 million people were dying. There is madness to this, perhaps, but one that may have been present for as long as art has played a role in human lives – since our ancestors braving the dark of the deepest caves to paint images on cold stone walls.

LOSS AS PERFORMANCE ART

This book has told the story of lost art, but there have also been lost artists. One cannot help but wonder what might have been painted had Giorgione not died at the age of thirty-two, or Raphael at thirty-seven. One cannot help but wring one's hands over how much time Velázquez spent busying himself at court relegating art almost to a hobby in order to maintain an elevated social position. What might a talent like Vladimir

Bas Jan Ader in *Ocean Wave*; published in *Bas Jan Ader*, Bulletin 89 (Art & Project, Amsterdam, August 1975)

Tatlin (1885–1953) have wrought had he not been frightened into limiting himself to still life drawing by Stalin's 1934 declaration against abstract art?

Dutch conceptual artist Bas Jan Ader (1942–75)[12] spent most of his short life in the United States, working as a photographer and performance artist in Los Angeles. On 9 July 1975, he set off alone from Cape Cod, Massachusetts, in a tiny sailboat, aiming to cross the Atlantic from New England to England. It was to be a performance, called *In Search of the Miraculous*, and it would be his last. His vessel, a 4-metre (12 ft 6 in) 'Guppy 13', which he'd named *Ocean Wave*, was not intended for transoceanic voyages and was the smallest craft in which an attempt to cross the Atlantic had ever been made. The performance began with a choir singing sea shanties around a piano in the gallery of his Los Angeles dealer, and was to end with another sing-along at Falmouth, in southern England, about two and a half months later. The central element of the performance was the voyage.

After three weeks, radio contact with the Ader ceased. Ten months later, on 18 April 1976, *Ocean Wave* was spotted 240 kilometres (150 miles) off the coast of Ireland, bobbing vertically in the waves, empty. The boat had been spotted 97 kilometres (60 miles) off the New England coast and again passing the Azores, but those were the only two sightings. It was recovered by a Spanish fishing boat and towed to the town of Coruña, from which it was stolen sometime between 18 May and 6 June 1976.

Ader is assumed to have drowned. Did he intend this voyage to be suicide-as-performance-art? Or was he convinced he could make the crossing, ill advised though it was in such a vessel and alone, and was simply overcome by the sea? Or did he, just maybe, deliberately create the most literal work of 'lost' art?

NOTES & INDEX

NOTES

INTRODUCTION

1   The Leonardo and Caravaggio numbers for documented works are generally agreed, but the figures for lost works are debated among scholars. For Caravaggio, Danielle Carrabino, a Caravaggio specialist, suggests eight lost paintings; John T. Spike, in contrast, believes the artist was more prolific and that some 115 canvases are lost (see his *Caravaggio*, Abbeville Press, 2010).

2   http://www.telegraph.co.uk/culture/art/leonardo-da-vinci/8875031/Did-Leonardo-da-Vinci-paint-the-Salvator-Mundi.html

3   A conclusion based on interviews with those involved, undertaken during research for Ingrid D. Rowland and Noah Charneuy, *Collector of Lives: Giorgio Vasari and the Invention of Art* (W. W. Norton, 2017), which is framed by the story of this lost Battle of Anghiari.

THEFT

1   http://www.bloomberg.com/news/articles/2015-04-27/a-186-million-rothko-pits-russian-tycoon-against-art-merchant

2   For more on Victorian art theft, and on this case in particular, see Noah Charney and John Kleberg, 'Victorian Art Theft in England: Early Cases and the Sociology of the Crime', *Journal of Art Crime* (Fall 2013), 19–30.

3   Information from the US Department of Justice and the US National Central Bureau of Interpol was posted in 2012 here, http://www.justice.gov/usncb/programs/cultural_property_program.php, but it has since been redacted after renovation of the website. The facts about art crime come from the UK National Threat Assessment, conducted by the UK's Serious Organized Crime Agency (SOCA). The rankings, which were classified, were provided by Scotland Yard and submitted in a report dated 2006, which report remained in the Threat Assessment for several years. Terrorist links to the Middle East come from the Interpol Tracking Task Force in Iraq and were reported at the annual Interpol Stolen Works of Art meeting in Lyon in either 2008, after meetings held in Lyon, Amman and Washington, DC. The head of Interpol Baghdad claimed to have proof of the link between Islamic terrorist groups and art crime (primarily antiquities looting). All the major players, from Interpol to the US Department of Justice, believed the report regarding the ranking of art crime in relation to drugs and the arms trade, and still broadcast its claims; there is no reason to doubt it, even though the details are still classified.

4   Information from interviews with Colonel Giovanni Pastore and Colonel Luigi Cortellessa, former and current Vice-Commandants of the art squad of the Carabinieri (the Italian military force charged with police duties), and from the annual yearbook published by the Carabinieri for internal distribution and for the media.

5   https://www.theguardian.com/world/2000/dec/23/arttheft.art

6   https://www.crimemuseum.org/crime-library/robberies/swedish-art-heist/

7   Mark Durney, 'Reevaluating Art Crime's Famous Figures', *International Journal of Cultural Property*, vol. 20/2 (May 2013), 221–32.

8   http://www.independent.ie/opinion/analysis/two-priceless-art-treasures-still-lie-buried-in-mountains-26243113.html

9   See Peter Watson, *The Caravaggio Conspiracy* (Penguin, 1985), for the complete story.

10 Some claim that the works were shopped around on the black market in the Philadelphia area in the early 2000s, but this is unconfirmed.

11 https://www.bostonglobe.com/metro/2015/03/17/gardner-museum-art-heist-one-boston-most-enduring-mysteries-years-later/9U3tp1kJMa4Zn4uClI1cdM/story.html

12 John Ruskin, *Pre-Raphaelitism and Other Essays* (London, 1906), 8.

13 Marion True and Kenneth Hamma, *A Passion for Antiquities* (Getty, 1994). For information on looted art in the Fleischman collection, see http://lootingmatters.blogspot.si/2008/01/some-reunited-fresco-fragments.html.

WAR

1 This story is told in many sources, but the most detailed rendition appears in Vera Schwarcz's *Place and Memory in the Singing Crane Garden* (University of Pennsylvania Press, 2008).

2 Quotes drawn from Chris Bowlby, 'The Palace of Shame that Makes China Angry', *BBC Magazine* (2 Feb 2015), http://www.bbc.com/news/magazine-30810596.

3 Geremie Barme, 'The Garden of Perfect Brightness, a Life in Ruins, *East Asian History* (June 1996), 118.

4 Garnett Joseph Wolseley, *Narrative of the War with China in 1860; to which is added the Account of a Short Residence with the Tai-ping Rebels at Nanking and a Voyage from thence to Hankow* (Longman, 1862), 226.

5 Quoted in Bowlby 2015, note 2 above.

6 Chris Buckley, Didi Kirsten Tatlow, Jane Perlez and Amy Qin, 'Voices from China's Cultural Revolution', *The New York Times* (16 May 2016).

7 http://www.oxfordtoday.ox.ac.uk/opinion/loot-chinas-old-summer-palace-beijing-still-rankles

8 Walter Scott, *Life of Napoleon Bonaparte, Emperor of the French*, vol. 1 (J. J. Harper, 1827), 362.

9 *Iliad*, Book I, ll.528–30. There is also a possibly apocryphal story that the 'beloved' of Phidias, a boy who had won the wrestling competition at the 86th Olympiad, was immortalized in the statue. Phidias is said to have carved the words *Pantarkes kalos* ('Pantarkes is beautiful') into Zeus' finger, along with a relief of the boy at the foot of the statue.

10 See Janette McWilliam, et al., *The Statue of Zeus at Olympia: New Approaches* (Cambridge Scholars Publishing, 2011), 44.

11 Livy, *Ad Urbe Condita* XLV, 28.5, and Dio Chrysostom, *Oratories* 12.51.

12 Pausanias, *Description of Greece*, 5.11.

13 Lucian, *Timon the Misanthrope*.

14 Cited in Georgius Cedrenus, *Historiarium Compendium* 322c.

15 Jozef Babicz, 'The Celestial and Terrestrial Globes of the Vatican Library, Dating from 1477, and Their Maker Donnus Nicolaus Germanus (ca.1420–ca.1490)', *International Coronelli Society for the Study of Globes* (June 1987), 155–68.

16 See Matthew Bogdanos, *The Thieves of Baghdad* (Bloomsbury, 2005), and Matthew Bogdanos, 'Thieves of Baghdad: and the Terrorists They Finance', in *Art Crime: Terrorists, Tomb Raiders, Forgers and Thieves*, ed. Noah Charney (Palgrave, 2016), 118–31.

17 Some twelve years later, Jenny Steiner's sister, Aranka Munk, commissioned Klimt to paint a posthumous portrait of her own daughter, Ria, who had killed herself in December 1911 after a break-up with her lover. Klimt was first asked to make a deathbed portrait of Ria, and the Munks rejected his first two attempts. The first is lost, but the second was adapted and transformed into *Die Tanzerin*. A 1917 version, entitled *Portrait of Ria Munk III*, survives in a private collection.

18 This story is told in Noah Charney, *Stealing the Mystic Lamb: The True Story of the World's Most Coveted Masterpiece* (Public Affairs, 2010)

19 Quoted in https://www.theguardian.com/artanddesign/2008/may/07/art

20 https://www.theguardian.com/artanddesign/2013/nov/05/picasso-matisse-nazi-art-munich

21 See Charney, *Stealing the Mystic Lamb*, note 18 above.

22 D. Grimaldi, 'Pushing Back Amber Production', *Science* 326 (2009), 51–52.

23 Pliny the Elder, *Natural History* 37.11.

24 Quoted in http://articles.latimes.com/2003/may/31/entertainment/et-holley31, from Theophile Gautier, *Voyage en Russie* (Paris, 1866).

25 Catherine Scott Clark and Adrian Levy, *The Amber Room: The Fate of the World's Greatest Lost Treasure* (Walker and Co., 2004); quoted in http://www.versopolis.com/panorama/211/stolen-beauty.

26 The most complete story of the Amber Room is told in C. Scott-Clark and A. Levy, *The Amber Room* (Atlantic, 2004).

27 https://www.forbes.com/forbes-life-magazine/2004/0329/048.html

28 Richard Spencer, 'Chinese Fury at Yves Saint-Laurent Art Sale, *The Telegraph* (3 Nov 2008), http://www.telegraph.co.uk/news/worldnews/asia/china/3373996/Chinese-fury-at-Yves-Saint-Laurent-art-sale.html

29 Terri Yue Jones, 'Two Bronze Animal Heads, Stolen 153 Years Ago, Returned to China, Reuters (28 June 2013); http://www.reuters.com/article/us-china-sculptures-idUSBRE95R0HW20130628

ACCIDENT

1 See Trevor J. Dadson, 'The Assimilation of Spain's Moriscos: Fiction or Realit*y?*', *Journal of Levantine Studies* 1: 2, Winter 2011, 11–30.

2 For more on this incident and what was lost, see Steven N. Orso, *Philip IV and the Decoration of the Alcázar of Madrid* (Princeton University Press, 1986).

3 The story of Cleopatra's Needle appears in numerous sources, but particularly good is Edward Chaney, 'Roma Britannica and the Cultural Memory of Egypt: Lord Arundel and the Obelisk of Domitian', in *Roma Britannica: Art Patronage and Cultural Exchange in Eighteenth Century Rome*, ed. D. R. Marshall, S. M. Russell and K. E. Wolfe (British School at Rome, 2011), 147–70. See also fascinating photographs of the building of the cylinder and pontoon in Ian Pearce, 'Waynman Dixon: In the Shadow of the Needle', in *Souvenirs and New Ideas*, ed. D. Fortenberry (Oxbow Books, 2013), 129–41.

4 A time capsule was buried beneath the obelisk in 1878, containing a box of cigars, another of hairpins, some pipes for tobacco, a baby bottle, a razor, a hydraulic jack (to demonstrate Victorian engineering), a three-foot (91-cm) tall bronze statue of the monument, an Indian rupee, a portrait of Queen Victoria, a text that related the story of its transport, the Bible in several languages, imperial weights, children's toys, British coins, a railway guide, a map of London, ten daily newspapers, the Biblical passage John 3:16 written out in 215 languages, and photographs of twelve famously beautiful British women (among which a photograph of Queen Victoria was not said to have been included).

5 A good summary of the *Vrouw Maria* wreck can be found at https://seanmunger.com/2014/10/09/the-story-of-the-vrouw-maria-the-lost-ship-of-incredible-dutch-art-treasures/.

6 Information provided by Riikka Köngäs, a Finnish conservator.

7 Raphael Minder, 'Historian Donates Velázquez to Prado', *New York Times* (15 December 2016).

8 Quoted in *Gentleman's Magazine*, vol. 20 (August 1843), 126.

9 https://www.thenation.com/article/painter-our-time/

10 Ariane Ruskin Batterberry, *17th and 18th Century Art* (McGraw-Hill, 1969), 71.

11 http://www.bbc.com/culture/story/20150320-the-worlds-first-photobomb

12 https://www.theguardian.com/culture/2003/aug/23/art

ICONOCLASM & VANDALISM

1 For this story, see Noah Charney, *The Art of Forgery* (Phaidon, 2015), 11–13.

2 Don Meredith, *Varieties of Darkness: The World of the English Patient* (Hamilton Books, 2012), 23.

3 Agostino Lapini, *Diario Fiorentino* (1596), cited in numerous modern sources, including http://www.publicartaroundtheworld.com/Fountain_of_Neptune.html

4 http://www.nytimes.com/1991/09/15/world/michelangelo-s-david-is-damaged.html

5 https://www.theguardian.com/world/2005/oct/17/arts.italy

6 *Ibid.*

7 Savonarola's story is widely told. Among the most complete histories is Donald Weinstein, *Savonarola: The Rise and Fall of a Renaissance Prophet* (Yale University Press, 2011).

8 Stephanie Barron, *Degenerate Art: The Fate of the Avant-Garde in Nazi Germany* (Abrams, 1991), 46.

9 'Al-Azhar Releases Fatwa Forbidding the Destruction of Artefacts', http://www.azhar.eg/observer-en/al-azhar-releases-fatwa-forbidding-the-destruction-of-artefacts

10 http://www.un.org/press/en/2015/
sc11775.doc.htm

11 http://www.fatf-gafi.org/media/fatf/
documents/reports/Financing-of-the-
terrorist-organisation-ISIL.pdf

12 Matthew Bogdanos, 'Illegal Antiquities
Trade Funds Terrorism', *CNN World*
(7 July 2011): http://articles.cnn.com/2011-
07-07/world/iraq.looting.bogdanos_1_
antiquities-trade-iraq-s-national-
museum-looting?_s=PM:WORLD

13 'Kunst als Terrorfinanzierung', *Der
Spiegel* 29, 2005: http://www.spiegel.de/
spiegel/print/d-41106138.html

14 *Blood Antiques*, produced by Journeyman
Pictures (2009).

15 Mogens Trolle Larsen, *The Conquest of
Assyria* (Routledge, 2014).

16 http://www.independent.co.uk/news/
world/middle-east/isis-militants-
nimrud-northern-iraq-destroy-3000-
year-old-city-archaelogists-ancient-
palace-islamic-a7512526.html

17 James Grantham Turner, 'Marcantonio's
Lost *Modi* and Their Copies', *Print
Quarterly* XXI (December 2004), 369–79.
See also *Art and Love in Renaissance
Italy*, exh. cat., Metropolitan Museum of
Art, New York (2008), cat. no. 99, 200–2.
For a comprehensive survey of the
engravings and their context, see Bette
Talvacchia, *Taking Positions: On the
Erotic in Renaissance Culture* (Princeton
University Press, 1999).

18 Diane deGrazia Bohlin, *Prints and
Related Drawings by the Carracci Family*
(Washington, DC: National Gallery of
Art, 1979).

19 Jonathon Green and Nicholas J.
Karolides, *Encyclopedia of Censorship*
(Facts on File, 2014), 20.

ACTS OF GOD

1 Pliny the Younger, *Letters* 6.16 and 6.20.

2 Suetonius and Tacitus both refer to the
second earthquake in writings about the
life of Nero, who was emperor at the time.

3 *Complete Works of Seneca the Younger*
(Delphi Classics, 2014), section XXVII: 4.

4 Over the last 17,000 years, Vesuvius
has erupted eight times. Following the
Plinian eruption of AD 79, the most active
period began in 1631. A serious eruption
killed 100 people in 1906, and the most

recent eruption took place in 1944,
destroying Allied airplanes and damaging
a local air base during the Second World
War; see www.geology.com/volcanoes/
vesuvius.

5 http://www.express.co.uk/
expressyourself/169599/Volcanoes-
Nature-s-nuclear-bombs

6 To date, some 1,500 corpses have been
found in excavations at Pompeii and
Herculaneum.

7 The idea that the statue straddled the
entrance to the harbour is based on a
misinterpretation of a mention by an
Italian traveller in 1395, who wrote
that the colossus watched 'over land
and sea'. This location at the harbour
is further challenged by some scholars,
including Ursula Vedder (*Der Koloss
von Rhodos. Archaologie, Herstellung,
und Rezeptionsgeschichte eines Antiken
Weltwunders*, Nunerich-Asmus Verlag
& Media, 2015), who suggests that it
was located ot the acropolis of the city,
a hill overlooking the harbour. For a good
account of this and the other wonders
of the ancient world, see Paul Jordan,
Seven Wonders of the Ancient World
(Routledge, 2014).

8 Strabo, *Geographica, xiv.2.5*

9 Pliny, *Natural History*, Book 34, xviii, 41.

10 *The Chronicles of Theophanes Confessor:
Byzantine and Near Eastern History*,
AD 284–813, ed. Cyril Mango and Roger
Scott (Clarendon Press, 1997), 481.

11 https://www.theguardian.com/
artanddesign/2008/nov/17/colossus-
rhodes-greece-sculpture; https://www.
theguardian.com/commentisfree/2015/
dec/27/greece-colossus-rhodes-new-project

12 Greek authors used the term *theamata*
to refer to the ancient 'wonders';
the work can better be translated as
'things to be seen'. Philo of Byzantium
wrote *On the Seven Wonders* in the
third century BC; his list excluded the
lighthouse at Alexandria but added
the walls of Babylon.

13 This story is told in many sources,
including 'L'Aquila Quake: Scientists See
Convictions Overturned': http://www.
bbc.co.uk/news/world-europe-29996872.

14 https://news.artnet.com/art-world/
appalling-restoration-destroys-giotto-
frescoes-at-the-basilica-of-saint-francis-
in-assisi-261811

15 http://www.repubblica.it/speciali/
arte/2015/02/19/news/assisi_allarme_
giotto_quel_restauro_una_minaccia_per_
gli_affreschi-107658385/

16 https://www.theguardian.com/
artanddesign/2015/feb/19/italian-art-
medieval-frescoes-damage

17 https://news.artnet.com/art-
world/giotto-chapel-damaged-by-
lightning-90009

18 Giorgio Vasari, 'Life of Giorgione', from
*Lives of the Most Eminent Painters,
Sculptors and Architects* (first published
1550), available in English translation
at http://members.efn.org/~acd/vite/
VasariGiorgione.html.

19 https://medium.com/@tylergreen/
giorgione-titian-and-or-cariani-
ec8e7446713e

20 *Ibid.*

21 http://www.pauldoughton.com/2012/02/
analysing-fondaco-dei-tedeschi-murals.html

22 https://www.nytimes.com/2016/11/06/
arts/design/after-the-florence-flood-
saving-vasaris-last-supper.html

23 Details of this event are described in
David Alexander, 'The Florentine Floods
– What the Papers Said', *Environmental
Management*, vol. 4, no. 1 (1980), 27–34.

24 The 14,000 number comes from
Christopher Clarkson, 'The Florence
Flood and Its Aftermath', *National
Diet Library Newsletter* (2003), 15–16.
Most articles refer to around 1,500
artworks, including https://www.nytimes.
com/2016/11/06/arts/design/after-
the-florence-flood-saving-vasaris-last-
supper.html.

25 http://tuscantraveler.com/2014/
florence/tuscan-travelers-tales-the-1966-
florence-flood/

26 https://www.nytimes.com/2016/11/06/
arts/design/after-the-florence-flood-
saving-vasaris-last-supper.html

27 For a summary of the historical and
on-going rescue work following the flood,
see Helen Spande, ed., *Conservation
Legacies of the Florence Flood of 1966:
Proceedings from the Symposium
Commemorating the 40th Anniversary*
(Archetype Publications, 2009).

28 https://www.theguardian.com/
world/2016/nov/04/florence-flood-50-
years-on-the-world-felt-this-city-had-to-
be-saved

29 New techniques for removing the
mulberry paper were developed as part
of the Panel Paintings Initiative, funded
by the Getty Foundation, alongside work
by the Opificio delle Pietre Dure. See
https://www.nytimes.com/2016/11/06/
arts/design/after-the-florence-flood-
saving-vasaris-last-supper.html.

30 *Ibid.*

31 Vitruvius *De Architectura*, II.8.9; see
http://www.perseus.tufts.edu/hopper/

32 Eric Moorman, 'Destruction and
Restoration of Campanian Mural
Paintings in the 18th and 19th Centuries',
in Sharon Cather, *The Conservation
of Wall Paintings* (Getty Conservation
Institute, 1991), 87–102.

33 There are many sources that describe
the destruction and excavation of Pompeii.
See, for example, Antonio d'Ambrosio,
Discovering Pompeii (Electa, 1998 and
later editions).

34 Quotes from Corrado are drawn
from email interviews undertaken
in February 2017.

TEMPORAL WORKS

1 This account comes from personal
interviews with Ulay, but can also be
found in Dominic Johnson, *The Art of
Living: An Oral History of Performance
Art* (Palgrave MacMillan, 2015).

2 This event is described in Enid Welsford,
The Court Masque (1927), and elsewhere;
see also https://www.britannica.com/
biography/Philip-III-duke-of-Burgundy.

3 For more on this event, see Ingrid D.
Rowland and Noah Charney, *Collector
of Lives: Giorgio Vasari and the
Invention of Art* (W. W. Norton, New
York, 2017).

4 Giorgio Vasari, *Le Vite de' piu eccellenti
pittori, scultori ed architetti* (1550), vol. 1
(Milan, 1846), 50.

5 A three-dimensional reproduction of what it is imagined the structure of the *macchina* looked like was prepared by an Italian team; see http://www.3d-archeolab.it/portfolio-items/stampa-3d-macchina-vasariana-bosco-marengo/.

6 Giorgio Vasari, *Le Vite de' piu eccellenti pittori, scultori e architetti* (1550), vol. 1 (Milan, 1846), 50.

7 *Grafton's Chronicle* (1569), quoted in numerous sources, including *Dictionnaire le Parisien* (http://dictionnaire.sensagent.leparisien.fr/FIELD%20OF%20THE%20CLOTH%20OF%20GOLD/en-en/).

8 Mentioned in Richard Grafton, *Grafton's Chronicle* (1569; reprinted 1809), vol. 2, 303–4.

9 There are numerous books on Christo and Jeanne-Claude's work, and basic information can be found on their website: http://www.christojeanneclaude.net/

10 http://www.nytimes.com/1991/10/28/us/christo-umbrella-crushes-woman.html

11 'Art: Homage to New York?', *Time*, 28 March 1960.

12 http://www.tate.org.uk/whats-on/tate-britain/exhibition/art-60s-was-tomorrow/exhibition-themes/destruction-art-symposium

13 Gustav Metzger, 'Machine, Auto-Creative and Auto-Destructive Art', *Ark* (Summer 1962).

DESTROYED BY OWNER

1 Leaves survive in collections in the UK at Chatsworth and Oxford, and in the Louvre, the Uffizi and the National Gallery of Art, Washington, DC (Carlo James, et al., *Old Master Prints and Drawings: A Guide to Preservation and Conservation* (Amsterdam University Press, 1997), 4). For a note on the Ghiberti collection, see Liana Cheney, *Giorgio Vasari's Teachers: Sacred & Profane Art* (Peter Lang, 2007), 250, note 10.

2 *Ibid.*

3 Oscar E. Vásquez, *Inventing the Art Collection: Patrons, Markets and the State in Nineteenth-Century Spain* (Penn State University Press, 2001), 54.

4 Pierre Cabanne, cited in Vásquez, note 3 above, 3.

5 *Ibid.*, 71.

6 Quoted in *Handbook to the Public Galleries of Art in or near London* (John Murray, 1845), 6, letter dated 1823.

7 *Ibid.*, 7.

8 This story is told in numerous sources, including Jonathan Black, *Winston Churchill in British Art, 1900 to the Present: The Titan with Many Faces* (Bloomsbury, 2017), 156–68. See also Hannah Furness, 'Secret of Winston Churchill's Unpopular Sunderland Portrait Revealed', *The Daily Telegraph* (10 July 2015), http://www.telegraph.co.uk/news/winston-churchill/11730850/Secret-of-Winston-Churchills-unpopular-Sutherland-portrait-revealed.html

9 *Ibid.* See also Sonia Purnell, *First Lady: The Life and Wars of Clementine Churchill* (Aurum Press, 2015).

10 Chris Wrigley, *Winston Churchill: A Biographical Comparison* (ABC-CLIO, 2002), 318.

11 For this and the quotes below, see Allison Keyes, 'Destroyed by Rockefellers, Mural Trespassed on Political Vision', *NPR* (9 March 2014).

12 Desmond Rochfort, *Mexican Muralists* (Chronicle Books, 1993), 126–7.

13 Sheila Wood Foard, *Diego Rivera* (Chelsea House Publishers, 2003), 9.

14 http://www.workers.org/2009/us/ford_hunger_march_0402/

15 Michael H. Hodges, 'Controversy Raged around Debut of Rivera's Murals', *Detroit News* (13 March 2015), http://www.detroitnews.com/story/news/local/wayne-county/2015/03/12/controversy-raged-around-debut-riveras-murals/70253934/.

16 Henry Adams, 'Detroit, 1932: When Diego Rivera and Frida Kahlo Came to Town', *The Conversation* (http://theconversation.com/detroit-1932-when-diego-rivera-and-frida-kahlo-came-to-town-38884).

17 http://www.artsjournal.com/culturegrrl/2007/01/dr_gachet_sighting_it_was_flot.html

18 Martin Bailey, 'Cezanne Joins Van Gogh for Close Scrutiny', *The Art Newspaper* (March 1999).

19   Carolyn Kleiner, 'Mysteries of History', *US News & World Report* (24 July 2000).

20   https://www.theguardian.com/world/2015/nov/13/russia-malevich-black-square-hidden-paintings

21   Bonnie Rimer, 'The Old Guitarist Meets New Technology', https://www.clevelandart.org/exhibcef/PicassoAS/html/7327426.html

22   http://www.openculture.com/2012/04/ithe_mystery_of_picassoi_landmark_film_of_a_legendary_artist_at_work_by_henri-georges_clouzot.html

23   Leonardo Klady, 'Return of the Centaur', *Film Comment*, no. 22, 20–22.

24   Richard Brettell, *Post-Impressionists* (Art Institute of Chicago and Abrams, 1987), 111–112.

25   Ulrike Knofel, 'A New Look at Works Destroyed by Gerhard Richter', *Der Spiegel* (3 Feb 2012).

26   Susan Stamberg, *For John Baldessari: Conceptual Art Means Serious Mischief* (NPR *Morning Edition*, 11 March 2013).

27   John Richardson, 'Rauschenberg's Epic Vision', *Vanity Fair* (September 1997), https://www.vanityfair.com/magazine/1997/09/rauschenberg199709

28   Holland Cotter, 'Robert Rauschenberg: North African Collages and Scatole Personali', *New York Times* (28 June 2012).

29   Vincent Katz, 'A Genteel Iconoclasm', *Tate Etc*, no. 8 (Autumn 2006).

30   Priscilla Frank, 'Artist Turns Abandoned Building Into Life-Sized Dollhouse … Then Burns It Down', *Huffington Post* (26 August 2014).

31   Vicki Goldberg, 'Ingres' Nude May Be Lost, But Her Afterimage Lingers', *New York Times* (21 September 2003).

32   http://www.wga.hu/frames-e.html?/bio/m/michelan/biograph.html. By contrast, Raphael, who was the epitome of *sprezzatura*, did not, as far as we know, try to destroy his drawings, and around 400 survive; see http://www.wga.hu/frames-e.html?/html/r/raphael/7drawing/index.html. Michelangelo lived much longer than Raphael (fifty-one years longer), however, and engaged in multiple art forms, including architecture. One can only wonder at the total number of drawings that Michelangelo must have made over his career, surely many thousands.

33   *Ibid.*, note 1 above, 136.

34   *Ibid.*, note 1 above, 13.

35   Carol Vogel, '$7 Million Michelangelo', *New York Times* (29 Jan 1998).

BURIED AND EXHUMED

1   The original text in Italian can be found here: http://vasari.sns.it/cgi-bin/vasari/Vasari-all?code_f=print_page&work=le_vite&volume_n=3&page_n=127

2   Susan B. Puett and J. David Puett, *Renaissance Art & Science @ Florence* (Truman State University Press, 2016).

3   http://www.atlasobscura.com/places/stufetta-del-bibbiena

4   http://www.slate.com/articles/life/welltraveled/features/2011/vatican_inside_the_secret_city/vatican_guide_the_pope_s_pornographic_bathroom.html

5   See Federico Zeri et al., *Italian Paintings: Sienese and Central Italian Schools* (Metropolitan Museum of Art, 1973).

6   See Lynn Catterson, 'Michelangelo's Laocoon?', *Artibus et Historiae* 26, no. 52, (2005), 29–56.

7   Quoted in http://www.spectator.co.uk/2011/09/medieval-frescoes/. See *Gli affreschi dell'Aula gotica nel Monastero dei Santi Quattro Coronati: Una storia ritrovata* (Skira, 2006).

8   The story is told in http://www.thedailybeast.com/articles/2015/04/05/the-fabulous-art-trove-saved-from-the-nazis-and-hidden-from-you.html. See also http://www.artnet.com/magazineus/features/darcy/darcy1-10-07.asp, and https://m.youtube.com/watch?list=PLxbMnBfiy6iF8-Bpca7VoY8LpebVQ93ot&v=GG-H93EILtU. Further information is provided by Miodrag Ćertić, director of the documentary film *The Mysterious Mr Šlomović* (2016).

9   Momo Kapor, *Dosije Šlomović* (Knjiga-Komerc, 2004).

10   http://www.cam.ac.uk/research/news/whale-tale-a-dutch-seascape-and-its-lost-leviathan

11   https://news.artnet.com/exhibitions/carnegie-conservators-reveal-true-face-of-medici-portrait-52064

12 http://www.csmonitor.
com/1984/0215/021509.html
13 https://www.theguardian.com/
artanddesign/2011/sep/20/xrays-
uncover-painting-goya-masterpiece
14 See A. H. Lanyard, *Nineveh and Its
Remains* (John Murray, 1849).
15 https://www.theguardian.com/
artanddesign/jonathanjonesblog/2015/
nov/20/asylum-artefacts-paris-
terrorists-louvre-isis
16 Josie Ensor, 'Previously Untouched
600 BC Palace Discovered Under Shrine
Demolished by Isil in Mosul', *The Daily
Telegraph* (2 March 2017);
http://www.telegraph.co.uk/news/2017/
02/27/previously-untouched-600bc-
palace-discovered-shrine-demolished/
17 *Ibid.*

LOST, OR NEVER WAS?

1 Translation by E. P. Coleridge
(George Bell and Sons, 1891).
2 Ribert Ingpen and Michael Page,
*The Encyclopedia of Things that
Never Were* (Penguin Studio, 1998).
3 http://edition.cnn.com/2015/04/21/
world/real-indiana-jones-lost-mayan-
cities/
4 Noah Charney, 'Space Archaeology',
Plugin Magazine (Summer 2016);
see also http://www.wired.co.uk/article/
scanning-the-past.
5 Juan Rodriguez Freyle, *El Carnero* (1638).
6 That account is told in Raleigh's own
account of his travels, *The Discoverie
of the Large, Rich and Bewtiful Empyre
of Guiana* (1596).
7 See, among many similar
announcements, http://www.ancient-
origins.net/news-history-archaeology/
huge-ancient-greek-city-found-
underwater-aegean-sea-003709.
8 See R. Hackforth, 'The Story of Atlantis:
Its Purpose and Its Moral', *Classical
Review* 58: 1 (1944), 7–9.
9 The excavations were published in
exemplary detail in the five-volume
series, *The Palace of Minos at Knossos*
(Macmillan, 1921–35).
10 http://www.independent.co.uk/
arts-entertainment/architecture/
has-the-original-labyrinth-been-
found-1803638.html

11 For more on this, see Irving Finkel,
Babylon: City of Wonders (British
Museum Press, 2008).
12 See Stephanie Daley, 'Ancient
Mesopotamian Gardens and the
Identification of the Hanging Gardens
of Babylon Resolved', *Garden History*
21:7 (1993).
13 Thomas M. Charles-Edwards, 'The
Arthur of History', in *The Arthur of the
Welsh* (University of Wales Press, 1991).
14 For more on the Turin Shroud, see Noah
Charney, *The Art of Forgery* (Phaidon,
2015), 229–32.
15 See Roger Sherman Loomis, *The Grail:
From Celtic Myth to Christian Symbol*
(Princeton University Press, 1991).
16 http://www.telegraph.co.uk/news/
worldnews/1311985/Colosseum-built-
with-loot-from-sack-of-Jerusalem-
temple.html
17 Cicero, *Pro Flacco* (In Defense of
Flaccus), 59 BC.
18 From the chapter on the life of Leonardo
da Vinci in Giorgio Vasari, *Lives of the
Most Eminent Painters, Sculptors and
Architects* (1568 edition).
19 The most thorough text on the Three
Sacred Treasures is Vyjayanthi R.
Selinger, *Authorizing the Shogunate:
Ritual and Material Symbolism in the
Literary Construction of Warrior Order*
(Brill, 2013). See also Stephen Turnbull,
Samurai: The World of the Warrior
(Osprey, 2006).
20 *Kido Koichi nikii* (Daigaku Shuppankai,
1966), 1120–1.
21 Rudolf Virchow, preface to Heinrich
Schliemann, *Ilios: City and Country
of the Trojans* (John Murray, 1880), xv.
22 Schliemann, *Troja und seine Ruinen*
('Troy and Its Ruins') (1885), 277.
23 Kenneth W. Harl, *Great Ancient
Civilizations of Asia Minor,* recorded
for The Teaching Company. Much of this
story is analyzed in Susan Heuck Allen,
*Finding the Walls of Troy: Frank Calvert
and Heinrich Schliemann at Hisarlik*
(University of California Press, 1999)
and Joachim Latacz, *Troy and Homer:
Towards a Solution of an Old Mystery*
(Oxford University Press, 2004).
24 See Heuck Allen, note 23 above, 259.

25 Blegen's excavations were published
   as *Troy: Excavations Conducted by the
   University of Cincinnati, 1932–38* (4 vols,
   Princeton University Press, 1950–8).
   His *Troy and the Trojans* (Praeger, 1963)
   is a popular version of his discoveries for
   non-specialists.
26 Rick Atkinson, 'Trojan Treasure
   Unlocks Art War', *The Washington Post*
   (6 September 1993).
27 For more on this, see Caroline Moorehead,
   The Lost Treasures of Troy (Weidenfeld
   and Nicolson, 1994).

CONCLUSION

1 A 32-minute film documenting its
  construction, and photographs of the
  work, will remain when it meets its
  ultimate end, though these ephemeral
  records are likely to be outlived by the
  basalt of which the spiral is formed
2 https://www.theguardian.com/
  books/2017/jan/31/burrow-franz-kafka-
  review-short-stories
3 https://www.nytimes.com/2017/02/
  20/arts/in-a-walt-whitman-novel-lost-
  for-165-years-clues-to-leaves-of-grass.
  html?_r=0
4 'Harper Lee Trade Frenzy and Concern
  Over New Book', *BBC News* (4 February
  2015); see also Lynn Neary, 'Harper Lee's
  Friend Says Author is Hard of Hearing,
  Sound of Mind', National Public Radio
  (5 February 2015). Through her lawyer,
  Lee released a statement that she was
  'delighted' to have found the manuscript
  and have it published, but there was
  sufficient concern that an investigation
  was launched in April 2015; it found the
  claims that Lee was taken advantage
  of to be unwarranted.
5 https://www.nextrembrandt.com/
6 The show ran in March 2017 at
  Liverpool's FACT and in May 2017
  at the Photographer's Gallery in
  London; *Material Speculations* has
  been exhibited in galleries worldwide.
  In 2016 Allahyari made available for
  download her research, her email
  correspondence with the Mosul
  Museum, which had held the destroyed
  works, high resolution images and
  3D-printable versions of each of
  the works; see http://rhizome.org/
editorial/2016/feb/16/morehshin-
allahyari/.
7 See http://www.bbc.co.uk/news/
  uk-36070721 and other news sites.
8 See Judith Bresler, 'Serra v. USA and
  its Aftermath: Mandate for Moral Rights
  in America?' in Daniel McClean, ed.,
  The Trials of Art (Ridinghouse, 2007),
  195–211.
9 The story is told in Stephen Turnbull
  and Wayne Reynolds, *Kawanakajima
  1553–64: Samurai Power Struggle*
  (Osprey, 2013).
10 See Jim Kurrach, 'Honjo Masamune
   and Important Missing Nihonto', in
   the newsletter of the Japanese Sword
   Society of Southern California, 1996.
11 https://news.artnet.com/art-world/
   stolen-willem-de-kooning-returned-
   1049207
12 http://www.basjanader.comw

Quintus Curtius Rufus 252, 253
—
rabbit head, from the Old
    Summer Palace *76*
Raimondi, Marcantonio 99–100,
    121–2
    I Modi (The Positions) 100,
    100, 105, 122–3, *123*, 126
Raphael 80, 99, 221, 224, 279
    *stufetta del Cardinal
    Bibbiena* 216–19
    Transfiguration 51, *54*
rat head, from the Old Summer
    Palace *75*
Rauschenberg, Robert, *Erased
    de Kooning* 202–3, *202*
Rembrandt van Rijn 271,
    271, 273
    Self-Portrait 26–7, *27*, 30
    Storm on the Sea of Galilee
    33, *34*, 36
Renoir, Pierre-Auguste 26–7,
    62, 198
    Bal du Moulin de la Galette
    194, 195
Riace Warriors *86*, 87
Ribera, Jusepe de 80
Richter, Gerhard 201
Rivera, Diego: *Detroit Industry*
    190–1, *192–3*
    *Man, Controller of the
    Universe 188–9*, 189–90
Rockefeller, John D. Jr 189–90
Romano, Giulio 100, 122, *123*
Rome, sack of (1527)
    58–9, 123
Royo, Josep, *World Trade
    Center Tapestry* 71
Rubens, Peter Paul 82
    Battle of Anghiari 17
    Battle of the Romans 80
    *Equestrian Portrait of
    Philip IV* 79
    Raising the Cross 51, *53*
    The Rape of the Sabines 80
Russborough House, Ireland 28
—
Saint-Laurent, Yves 75
Saito, Ryoei 194–5
Santi Quattro Coronati 226–30
Savonarola, Girolamo 18, 104,
    109–10, 113, 195
Schliemann, Heinrich 263–5
Schliemann, Sophia *265*
Second World War (1939–45) 8,
    60–2, 66–9, 71–4, 231, 266,
    278, 279

Serra, Richard, *Tilted Arc*
    274–5, *275*
Siculus, Diodorus 252–3
Signorelli, Luca 221
Šlomović, Erich 230–1
Smithson, Robert, *Spiral Jetty*
    269, *269*
Spencer, Georgiana 21, *22*, 41
Strabo 57, 133, 245, 252
Sutherland, Graham, *Winston
    Churchill* 186–8, *186*
Sylvester, Saint 226–30, *226–7*
—
Taliban 114, 115
Temple of Herod 257
Theodora, Empress 105, 107
Three Sacred Treasures of
    Japan 261–2
Tinguely, Jean: *Homage to New
    York* 173
    *Study for an End of the
    World* 173, *173*
Tintoretto 80
Titian 80, 122, 140, 143, 148
Trajan *10–11*, 12–13
Treasure of Priam 265–6, *265*
Troy 245–6, 263–6
—
Ulay: *Fototot* 175–6, *175*
    Fototot I 157–9, *158*, *159*
—
Van Gogh, Vincent:
    *Congregation Leaving
    the Reformed Church
    in Nuenen 31*, 32
    Portrait of Dr Gachet
    194–5, *194*, 207
    *View of the Sea at
    Scheveningen 30*, 32
Vasari, Giorgio 16, 110, 140
    collector of drawings 179
    Last Supper 146, *146*, 147
    Libro de' Disegni 179, *180*
    *The Lives of the Most
    Eminent Paints, Sculptors
    and Architects* 73, 101, 143,
    144, 213
    Macchina Grandissima
    162, *163*
    Michelangelo 170, 181, 205,
    207, 208
    Santo Maria Novella 213,
    215, 216
    secular relics 258, 259–60
    wedding of Cosimo de'
    Medici 161–2
Vásquez, Oscar 182, 183

Velázquez, Diego 279
    *The Expulsion of the
    Moriscos* 79, 92, *93*
    *Las Meninas (The
    Handmaidens)* 79, 80,
    92, 93–6, *95*, 279
    Portrait of Philip III
    92–3, *93*
Vermeer, Johannes 28
    The Concert 33, *35*
Veronese, Paolo 80
Vesuvius, Mount 129–30, *129*,
    149–50
Villa of Poppea, Oplontis 151,
    152–3
Volaire, Pierre-Jacques,
    Eruption of Vesuvius 129
Vrouw Maria 91–3
—
Watson, Peter 32
Weyden, Rogier van der:
    Deposition 8, *12*, 13–14
    *Justice of Trajan and
    Herkinbald* 8, 9–14, *10–11*
Whitehall Palace, London 81,
    82, 83
Whitman, Walt 270
Wilson, Sir William James
    Erasmus 89–90
Wolseley, Garnet Joseph 48–9
Wolsey, Cardinal 164–5, 168
Worth, Adam 18, 38, 39–43
Worth, John 40–2
—
Zeus 55, 57–8, 87, *87*, 133
zodiac water clock 47, 48, *48*,
    63, 75–6

PICTURE CREDITS

Phaidon Press Limited
Regent's Wharf
All Saints Street
London N1 9PA

Phaidon Press Inc.
65 Bleecker Street
New York, NY 10012

phaidon.com

First published 2018
© 2018 Phaidon Press Limited
Text © Noah Charney

ISBN 978 07148 7584 2

A CIP catalogue record for this book is available
from the British Library and the Library of
Congress.

Commissioning Editor: Diane Fortenberry
Production Controller: Sarah Kramer
Design: Hans Stofregen
Cover Design: Julia Hasting
Layout: Studio Chehade

Printed in China